WILD Washington

Animal Sculptures A to Z

Poems **Nancy Arbuthnot**

Illustrations **Cathy Abramson**

Foreword by E. Ethelbert Miller

The Annapolis Publishing Company
Annapolis, Maryland

Other books by Nancy Arbuthnot:

An American Artist in World War II: Jason Schoener at Eniwetok Atoll (art monograph), Needham Heights, MA: Simon & Schuster, 1994

Mexico Shining: Songs of the Aztecs (translations), Boulder, CO: Three Continents Press, 1994.

From Where the Wind Blows, (co-translation with the author, Le Pham Le), Sacramento, CA: The Vietnamese International Poetry Society, 2003.

Other books illustrated by Cathy Abramson:

Simple Secrets of Parenting: Easy as ABC, John Q. Baucom, Washington, DC: Child & Family Press, 1997.

All photography copyright as attributed.
All rights reserved.
© 2005 The Annapolis Publishing Company.
All rights reserved 2005.
Printed in the United States of America

No part of the contents of this book may be reproduced without the written permission of the publisher.
ISBN 1-884878-09-1

Library of Congress Cataloging-in-Publication Data
Abramson, Cathy Beth 1951–
Arbuthnot, Nancy Prothro 1950–
  Wild Washington: Animal Sculptures A to Z
  introduction by Cathy Abramson
  foreword by E. Ethelbert Miller
  poetry and text by Nancy Prothro Arbuthnot
  illustrations by Cathy Abramson

Includes bibliographic references
ISBN 1-884878-09-1

Cover Art: Perry Lions

The pair of lions at each end of the Taft Bridge on Connecticut Avenue over Rock Creek Park, one sleeping and one roaring, were sculpted in 1906 by Roland Hinton Perry (1870-1941). Perry is also known for having created *The Court of Neptune Fountain* at the Library of Congress. Molded out of precast concrete, the lions were restored once in 1964, then removed in 1993 for a complete recreation in high-strength concrete with stainless steel reinforcement. In 2000, the two lion pairs were reinstalled on their pedestals on the bridge, and two additional bronze casts were made for the entrance to the National Zoo. Local residents have named the lions Roland after the original sculptor and Reinaldo after the master sculptor of the renovation project.

Roland Hinton Perry, *Perry Lions*, 1906. Pre-cast concrete. Taft Bridge. Connecticut Avenue, NW.

Frontispiece: Vaquero

A rugged-faced Mexican vaquero (from Spanish for *vaca*, or cow) rides his steed with wild abandon in front of the National Museum of American Art. The brilliantly-colored fiberglass statue is the work of Luis Jimenez (b.1940) of Texas who combines high art and popular culture to create monumental sculptures that, as one critic notes, "both celebrate and question the mythic icons of his Hispanic heritage." The vaquero's horse is probably either a mustang or a quarter horse. The mustang (from Spanish for *mesca*, or mixture) is a feral horse found in herds on federal lands, and a descendent of the first horses brought by European explorers in the 16th century. The quarter horse, so named because it can run the quarter mile faster than other breeds, was once used for Pony Express mail delivery in the mid-19th century and it is still used in ranch work today.

Luis Jimenez, *Vaquero*, modeled 1980, cast 1990. Fiberglass. Smithsonian American Art Museum, 750 9th Street, NW.

Contents

Foreword
viii

Poems and Notes
1

Animal Sculpture Site Locations
78

Animal Sculpture Site Map
79

Zoonotes
80

Bibliography
109

Index: Sculptor/Architect
110

Index: Animals
111

Introduction

Washington, DC is a city of monumental sculptures that adorn the parks, bridges, and entrances to the nation's capital. Less well known are sculptures, friezes and decorative elements found on fountains, at the entrances to embassies, on rooftops, and along walkways and gardens. These are the little treasures that are part of Washington's unique urban landscape. Once you know that these gems exist, you will start noticing them all around you.

Finding the animals for an animal alphabet book meant exploring the city on foot. We began with the obvious: the lions and eagles, then the equestrian sculptures, all symbols of strength and power. Then we discovered the anteater, the bison, the crab. We began to see multiples of some sculptures (the concrete lions on the Taft Bridge and the bronze lions at the entrance to the National Zoo), and none representing other letters (alas, Washington lacks yaks). Some sculptures have lengthy histories such as the Triceratops (or Uncle Beazley), a favorite of Washington children for generations. It was first installed at the New York World's Fair in 1964, then moved in front of the Natural History Museum on the Mall, and finally came to rest near the rhinoceros exhibit at the National Zoo. Other sculptures have no obvious history, only a brief notation of sculptor and date of installation. We began to wonder why a particular sculpture was installed at a particular site and to ponder the relationship of the sculpture to its surroundings.

In the poems, Nancy Arbuthnot explores the relationship of each sculpture to the animal it represents and to its environment, both physical and temporal. The poetry begins as a puzzle, using the ancient form of riddle poems to examine this interplay. The sculptures were created from stone, bronze, concrete or fiberglass, sentinels of time and place; yet after reading the poems, you might notice a subtle change, as some sculptures seem to come alive. Is it a shifting of light, or of perspective or understanding?

The illustrations are a response to the poems and to the sculpture. They are an attempt to make frozen objects more real and alive. Perhaps the best description of the illustration technique used is *photo illustration.* The sculptures were photographed by Cathy Abramson from several different angles. The images were then imported into Adobe Photoshop where they were used as a background layer, or underdrawing. Layers of texture and line drawing were then superimposed. Often figures were drawn in and backgrounds altered to enhance each illustration in an attempt to move beyond simple documentation.

Integrating these three art forms – sculpture, poetry, and illustration – was itself a creative exercise. The sculpture of *The Spider* by Louise Bourgeois was described as maternal in the poem and menacing in the initial illustration. Although Bourgeois' writings reinforce the maternal aspects of the spider, the sculpture looms over the garden on angular, ropy legs. Both the poem and the illustration were rewritten and reworked to reflect these dual and dueling qualities.

Finally, *Wild Washington* is a guidebook. By taking a look at the map that follows the alphabet portion of the book and noting the exact location of the sculptures in the photo captions, you can take a walking tour of the stationary wildlife in several Washington neighborhoods. Read the poems and descriptions, and view the illustrations as you enjoy your own Washington safari.

Acknowledgements

I would like to thank E. Ethelbert Miller for his foreword and interest in our work. I would like to acknowledge the assistance of many museum curators and exhibit directors, especially at the National Zoo, and the often anonymous writers and researchers on Washington's buildings, monuments and sculptures; my largest debt is, of course, to James M. Goode for his invaluable resource, *The Outdoor Sculpture of Washington, DC: A Comprehensive Historical Guide* (Smithsonian Institution Press, 1974; second edition forthcoming). For granting me time free from teaching duties, I am grateful to the United States Naval Academy. For advice and encouragement, I want to thank my family and friends, especially my poetry group of many years – Geraldine Connolly, Christina Daub, Nan Fry, Patricia Gray, Jean Johnson, and Saundra Maley. I also very much appreciate Timothy Parker for his photographs of several sculptures *in situ*. Most especially, I am deeply appreciative of Cathy Abramson for her inspiring eye and artwork, her persistent good humor and dedication, and her wonderful spirit of collaboration.

–Nancy Arbuthnot

Foreword

I felt like Noah when I opened *Wild Washington*. I was curious to know which of God's creatures were included in this book. I smiled when I turned to the letter U and found the unicorn that sits in northwest Washington, overlooking Rock Creek Park. If you like surprises, *Wild Washington* will offer one on every page. This is the kind of book you want to grow old with.

Wild Washington embraces the long-term residents of this city, as well as its many visitors. It is an urban guidebook for the average American as well as the historian, visual artist, and poet. One will want to share this book with a friend; its design makes it a gift and small treasure.

Some people might want to memorize the poems written by Nancy Arbuthnot. It's another way of understanding a different Washington. I can see a poem taking the hand of a "shy" reader and directing him across town to view one of the sculptures. This is a fun book and easy to read as ABC. Just remember the W stands for whooping crane and *Wild Washington*.

> – *E. Ethelbert Miller*
> *Director, African American Resource Center*
> *Howard University*

For my children, Margaret, Charles and Annie
Nancy Arbuthnot

For my sons, David, Steven and Jonathan
Cathy Abramson

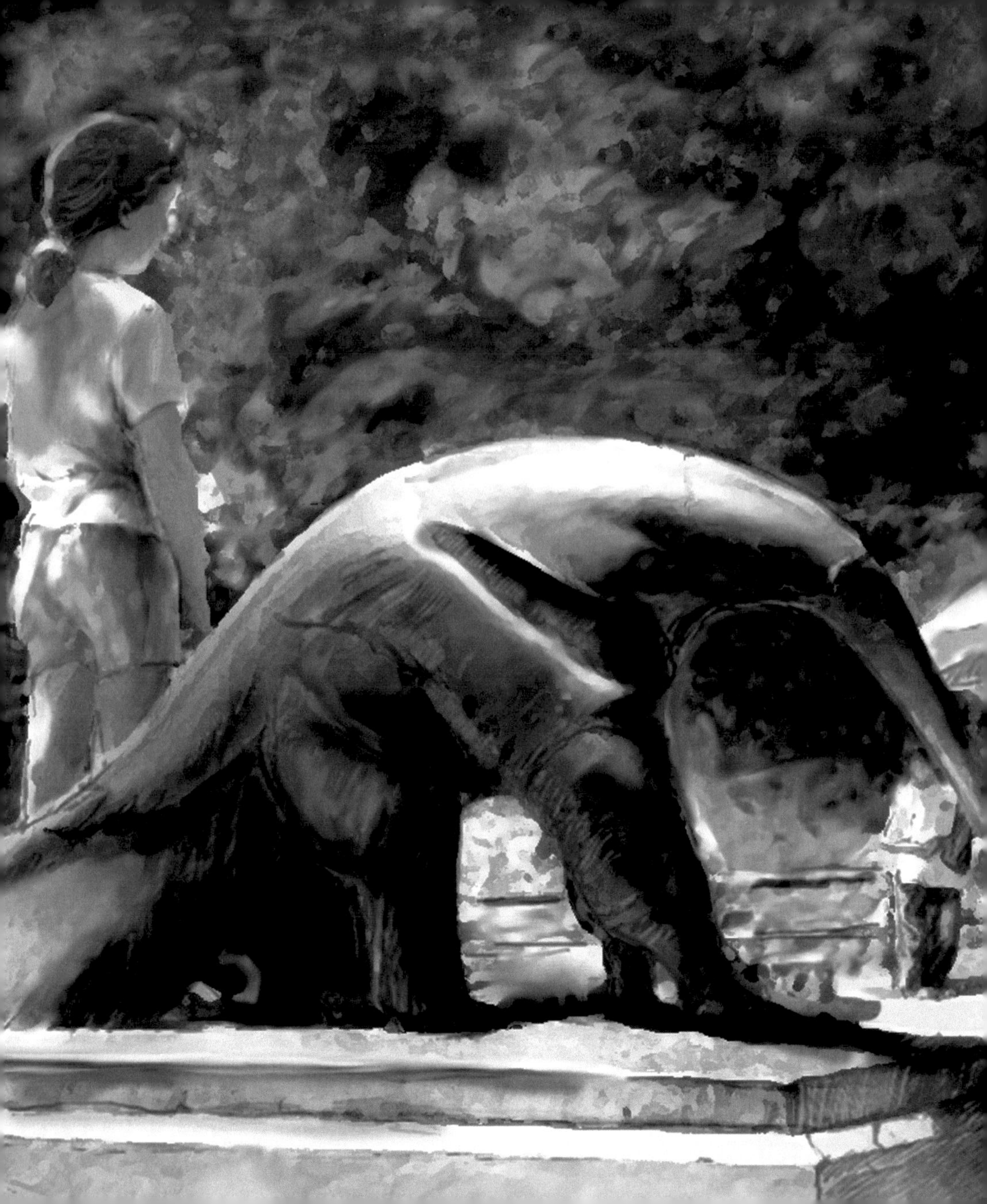

Anteater

With one great swipe
of its long curved claw
Myrmecophagidae
wrenches open
termite mounds,
whole ant-towns.
Nosing about
with long pointed snout,
tongue out,
it sucks the insects down.

This anteater
in contrast,
chiseled, zoo-tamed,
burnished by
innumerable stroking hands,
stares astonished
at ants marching across
its bronze paws.

Anteater

Erwin Frederick Springweiler (1896-1968), one of America's premier animal sculptors, was born in Germany and studied at the Art Craft School in Pforzheim before emigrating to the United States. His interest in animal sculpture was inspired by sculptors Paul Manship and Herbert Haseltine, with whom he studied early in his career. His work is on display at many zoos, including those in Washington and Detroit. Springweiler's life-size *Giant Anteater* was created under the aegis of the Public Works of Art Project.

Erwin Frederick Springweiler *Anteater*, 1938. Bronze. National Zoo, in front of the Small Mammal House.

The giant anteater of Central and South America boasts a long bushy tail, powerful forearms, a long snout, and small ears and eyes. It walks a slow shuffle on knuckles to protect its sharp claws. It rips open ant and termite mounds with its paw, scoops up the insects with its long, sticky tongue, and then, toothless and unable to chew, crushes its prey against its upper mouth. Its only natural predators are the puma and jaguar.

Bison

"I am eternally obsessed with two deep desires – one, to spend as much time as possible in the wilderness, and the other, to accomplish something worthwhile in art," wrote sculptor Alexander Phimister Proctor (1860-1950). His love of wilderness

Alexander Phimister Proctor, *Buffaloes*, 1914. Bronze. Q Street Bridge at 24th Street, NW.

was influenced by his childhood in Canada and Colorado, and his artistic talents were nourished at the Art Students League in New York and the Académie Julien in Paris. His four huge bronze bison, cast in 1914, watch over the Buffalo Bridge. These noble images of the endangered American wilderness were the largest bronzes ever cast in one piece in the US. Proctor's Princeton *Tiger* and University of Texas *Mustangs* also display his love of wild subjects.

The American bison, commonly called buffalo (a name correctly used for related hoofed animals of Asia and Africa) is the largest land animal in America since the Ice Age. Typically, bison weigh 2,000 pounds and stand six feet at the shoulder hump, where energy-rich fat is stored. Once bison ranged over most of North America in a vast herd of 30-70 million, travelling sometimes at speeds of 30-35 miles per hour. By the late 1800s, they were almost exterminated, leaving a wild population of only 1500. Now wild bison have been restored to the range in Yellowstone National Park, and Native American tribes and other groups have helped increase the numbers to over 350,000.

Bison

Once they forded rivers,
roamed the sweetgrass plains.
Now on this bridge
humming with cars
above the rocky creek
four bison rest, shaggy, heavy,
missing the smell of prairie rain.

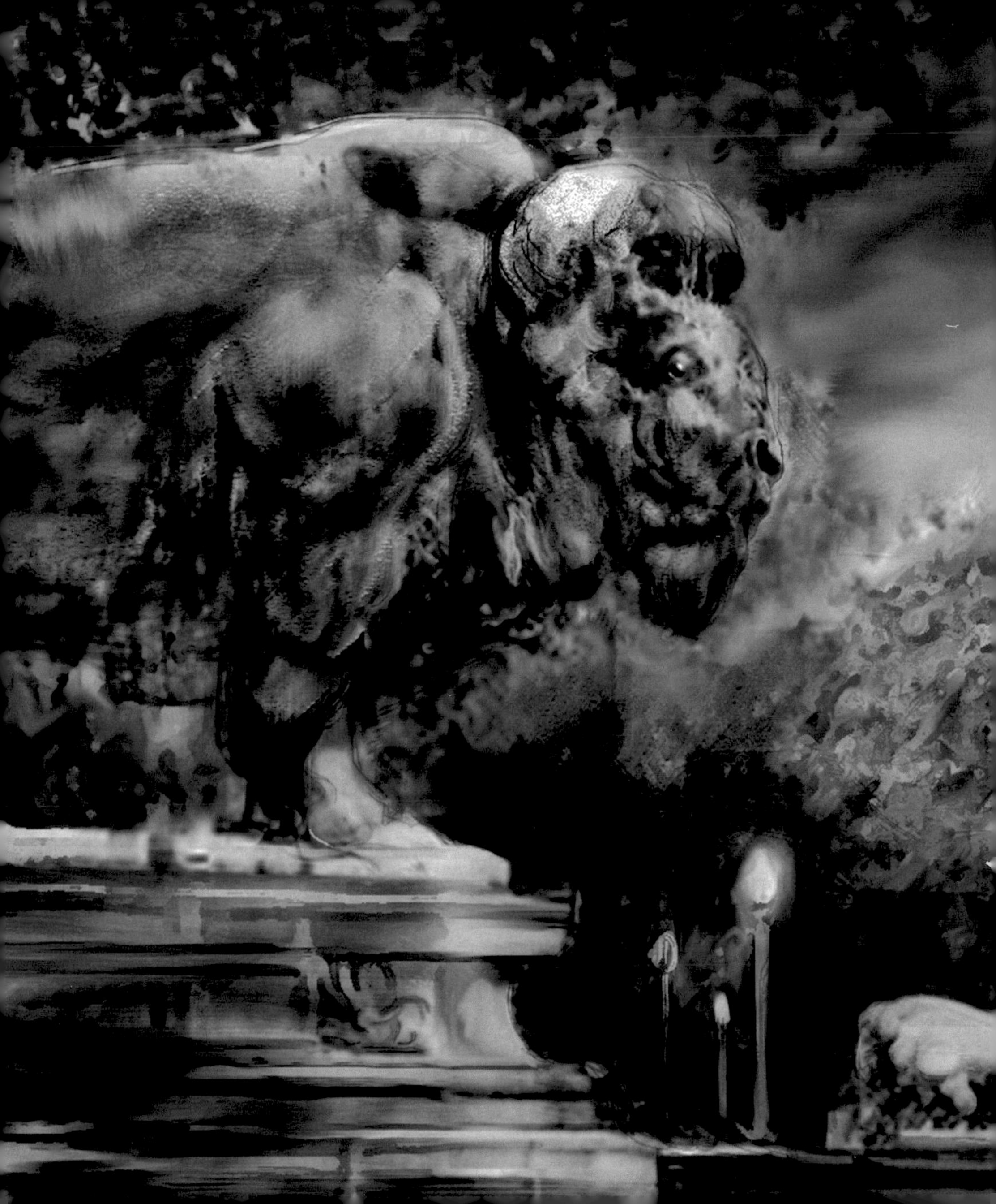

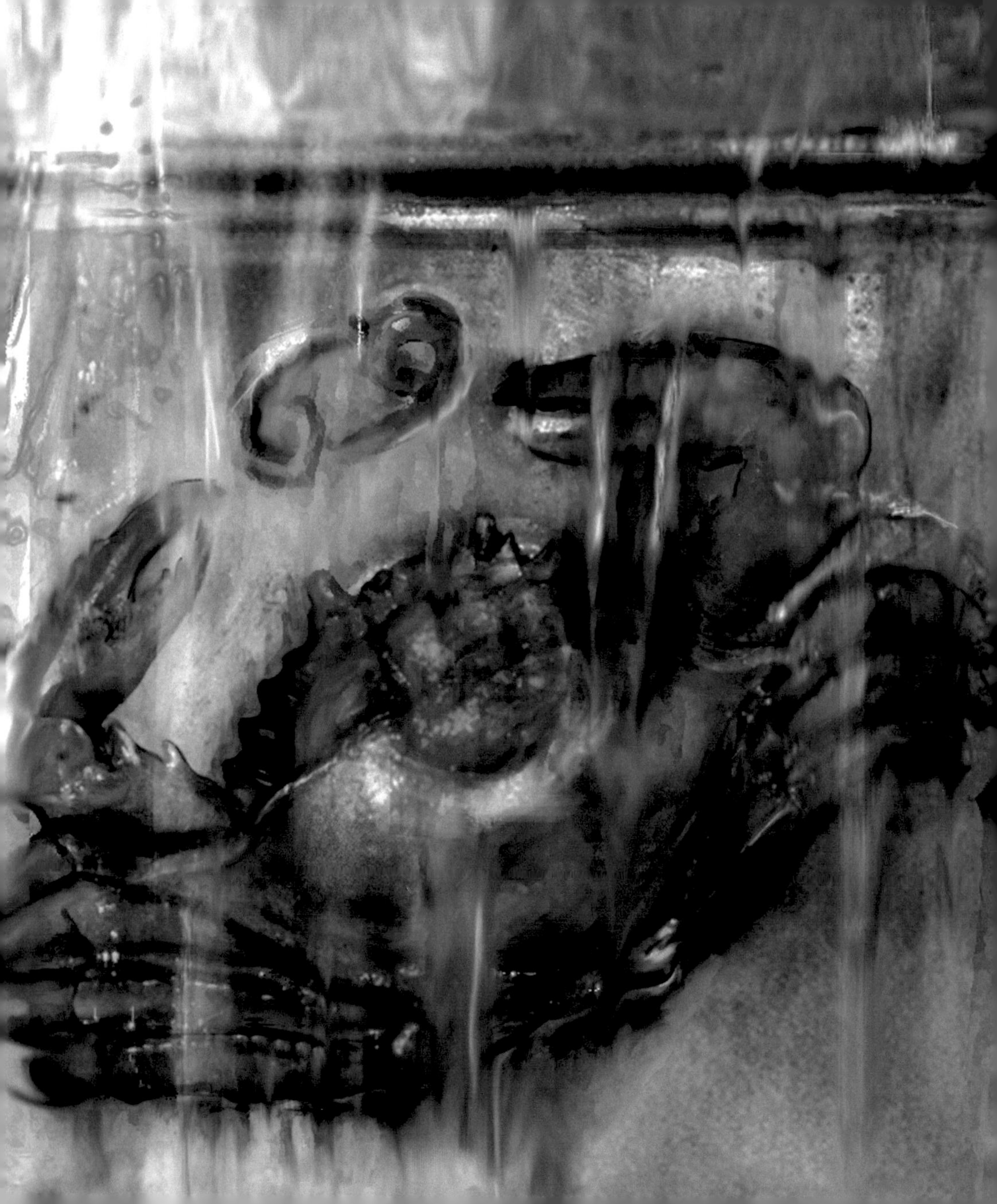

Crab

Between busy avenues,
this memorial fountain:
water cascading
over large bronze basins
into a low curbed pool of granite.

Zodiac signs circle
the basin: Aries
the Ram, Pisces the Fish,
Cancer the Crab.

Cars on the avenues
circle the fountain day
after day. Evening after
evening constellations swim
the sky, season after season.

Sidney Biehler Waugh, *Andrew W. Mellon Memorial Fountain,* 1952. Bronze and granite. Between Constitution and Pennsylvania Avenues near 10th Street, NW, across from the West Wing of the National Gallery of Art.

Crab

This crab is one of the twelve signs of the zodiac featured on the large circular *Andrew Mellon Memorial Fountain,* designed by architect Otto R. Eggers after a fountain in Italy as a tribute to Andrew W. Mellon (1855-1935), industrialist, financier, statesman and founder of the National Gallery of Art. Water cascades down three tiers of bronze basins to a low-curbed granite pool. The signs of the zodiac, designed by Sidney Biehler Waugh (1904-1963), circle the third basin, the largest fountain basin ever cast in bronze. A chief designer for Steuben Glass, Waugh was a noted sculptor of figural public works, including sculptures at the National Archives and the Federal Reserve Building.

The first known zodiacs date back to 5th century Mesopotamia, where animal signs representing constellations were recorded on clay tablets. The Greek astronomer Hipparchus brought the idea of the zodiac into the Greek world where the term "zodiac" (meaning animal signs) was first used. The ancient astronomer Ptolemy described the zodiac in *The Alamagest.* The crab, the sign for the constellation Cancer, appears as a minor character in Greek mythology. The goddess Hera sent a crab to attack Hercules as he was fighting the snake-haired Hydra. Although crushed by Hercules, the crab was rewarded by Hera with a place in the heavens.

The crab is an invertebrate crustacean with a flat shell, four pairs of legs, one pair of pincers, a pair of eyes on moveable stalks, and a pair of longer antennae. These creatures, sometimes terrestrial but chiefly marine, are omnivorous scavengers and, in some species, predators.

Dog

Timothy Parker

Neil Estern, *FDR and Fala*, 1997. Bronze. FDR Memorial, Ohio Drive and Independence Avenue, SW.

Franklin Delano Roosevelt's favorite pet, Fala (short for Murray of Falahill), a black Scottish terrier, performed tricks for White House guests (such as standing on his hind legs when the national anthem was played) and accompanied FDR just about everywhere. The Scottish terrier, originally bred in Scotland as a hunter of foxes and badgers, is a small, compact dog with short, heavy legs and erect ears and tail. Dependable and loyal, but independent and feisty, it bears the nickname, "Diehard."

In *FDR with Fala*, part of the larger FDR Memorial, Neil Estern (b. 1926) seeks to convey the personality of his subject as well as a recognizable portrait. FDR stipulated that he wanted no monument erected to him, and Estern's statue added to the memorial's controversy by concealing FDR's wheelchair with a long cape. But the memorial's open-air design and the soothing water sculpture create an inviting environment.

Dog

The poor and tired
line the wall for a new deal
after so many disasters.

Across the Tidal Basin
a voice echoes:
You have nothing to fear…

Ears perked, tail ready
to wag, Fala sits
in the open-air room

forever faithful
at the foot of his master.

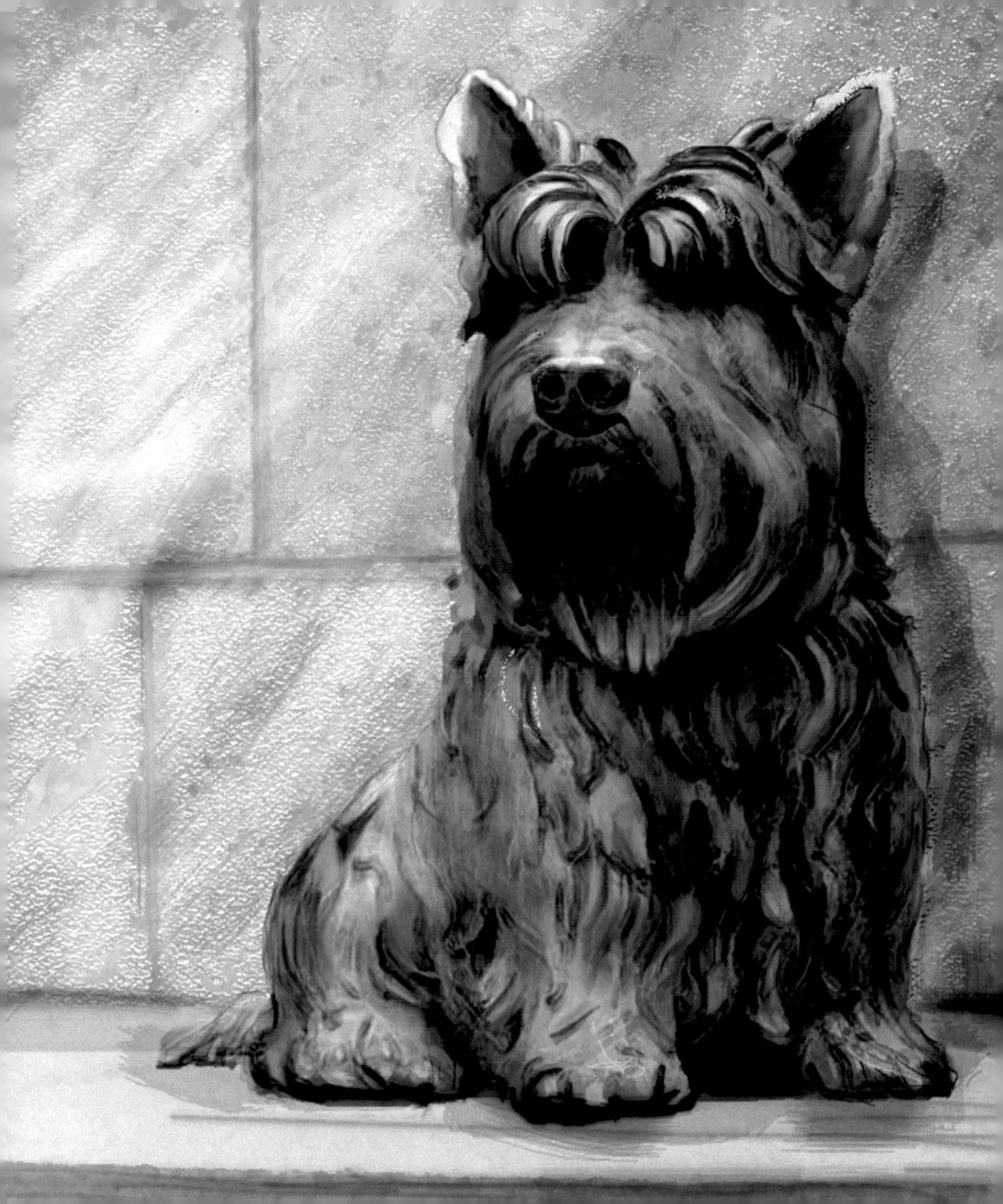

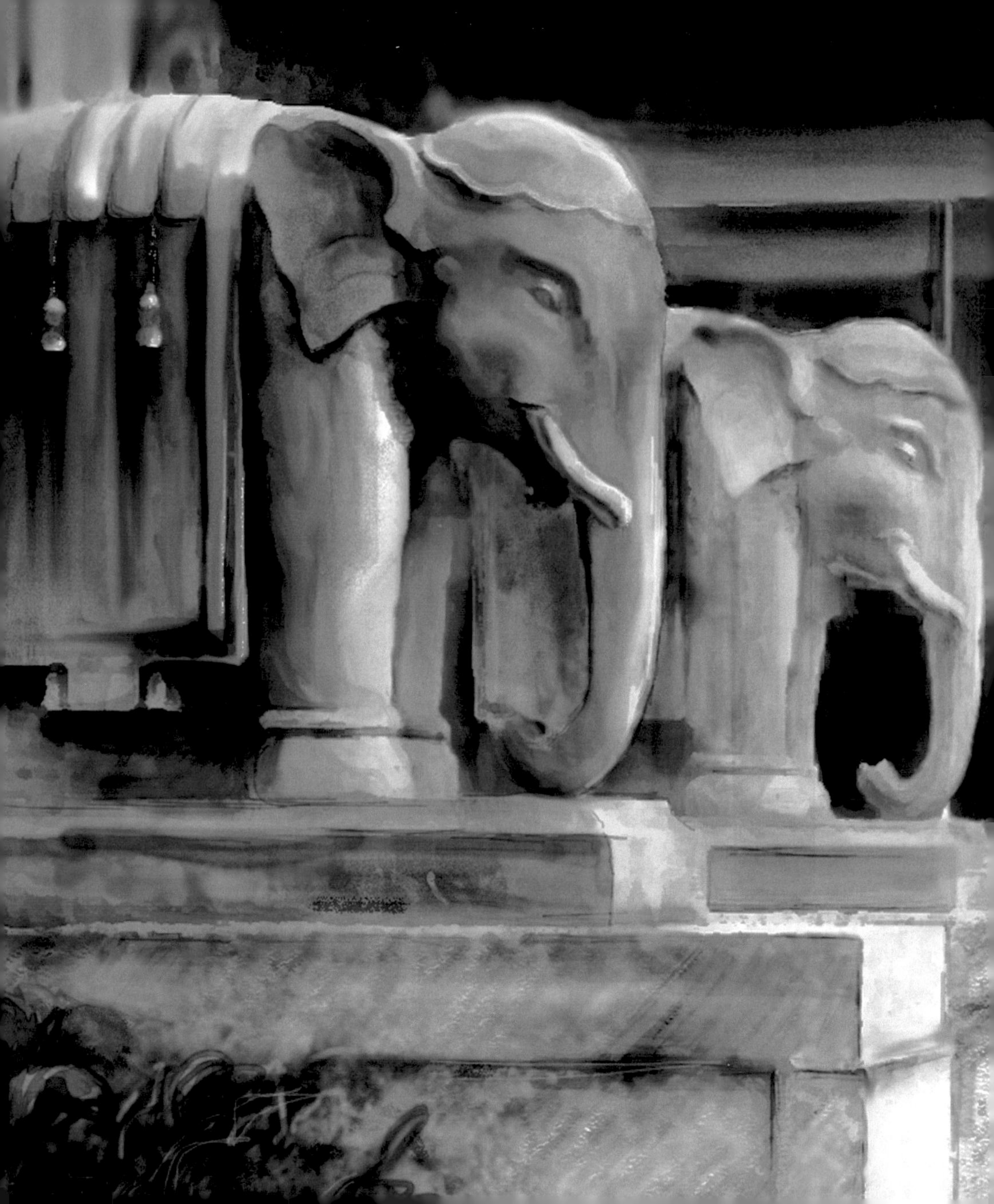

Elephant

Figures of sagacity
on the steps of the chancery,
two gray marble elephants
arrayed in bangled blankets
attend each passing dignitary.
The unknown sculptor's hand
has turned to sand.
Still the elephants stand.

Timothy Parker

Anonymous, *Elephants*, ca 1955. Marble. Indian Chancery, 2536 Massachusetts Avenue, NW.

Elephant

Two simple but dignified gray marble elephants flank the steps of the Indian Chancery on Massachusetts Avenue. A symbol of strength and wisdom, the elephant often appears in Indian temple architecture, especially as the figure of Ganesh, a god with human body and the head of an elephant.

The elephant, largest of the land mammals, is an extremely social animal, living in family groups headed by a female. The Asian, or Indian, elephant, somewhat smaller than the African elephant but with larger ears, reaches about 8 feet at the shoulder and weighs 4-6 tons. Its daily diet consists of hundreds of pounds of roots, grass, leaves, bark, bananas and sugar cane. Long domesticated, Asian elephants were once employed in logging and warfare, but are now used mainly for ceremonies and entertainment. Although it has few natural enemies, the elephant is in grave danger of extinction due to habitat loss and the poaching of male elephants for their ivory tusks.

Fawn

This gilded bronze nymph with fawn graces Judiciary Square as a memorial to lawyer Joseph Darlington. The sculptor, Carl Paul Jennewein (1890-1978), one of the foremost art deco sculptors in America, came to the US from Germany in 1907

Carl Paul Jennewein, *Joseph Darlington Fountain*, 1923. Gilded bronze. Judiciary Park, 5th and D Streets, NW.

and studied at the Art Students League in New York. Some of his most significant works include sculptures or sculptural friezes at the Rayburn Office Building, the Old Executive Office Building and the Department of Justice in Washington; the AT&T Building and RCA Building in New York; and the Philadelphia Museum of Art. Jennewein often based his sculpture on figures in Greek art and mythology; the Darlington Fountain sculpture evokes Diana, the Greek goddess of the hunt and protector of virgins who, in one myth, tries to prevent Hercules from capturing a doe and in another, turns Acteon, who has seen her bathing naked in a pool, into a stag. When friends objected to the nudity of the Darlington Fountain nymph, Jennewein is said to have replied that the figure was "direct from the hand of God instead of from the hands of a dressmaker." Controversy concerning his sculpture again surfaced in 2002 when the US Attorney General ordered two of Jennewein's semi-nude sculptures in the Justice Department Building to be draped.

Deer evolved about five million years ago, one group in North America and Siberia, the other in Asia. Male deer grow antlers, a bony growth covered by a skin called "velvet" that supplies oxygen and nutrients to the growing bone. Unlike horns, which continue to grow, antlers are shed each year after the mating season and regrown.

Fawn

Direct from the hands of God
proclaimed the sculptor
of his gilded bronze.

Gently the naked nymph of the fountain
lays her hand on the slender back
of the fawn,

while in the marble buildings all around
this green leafy shrine
justice thunders like a mighty river down.

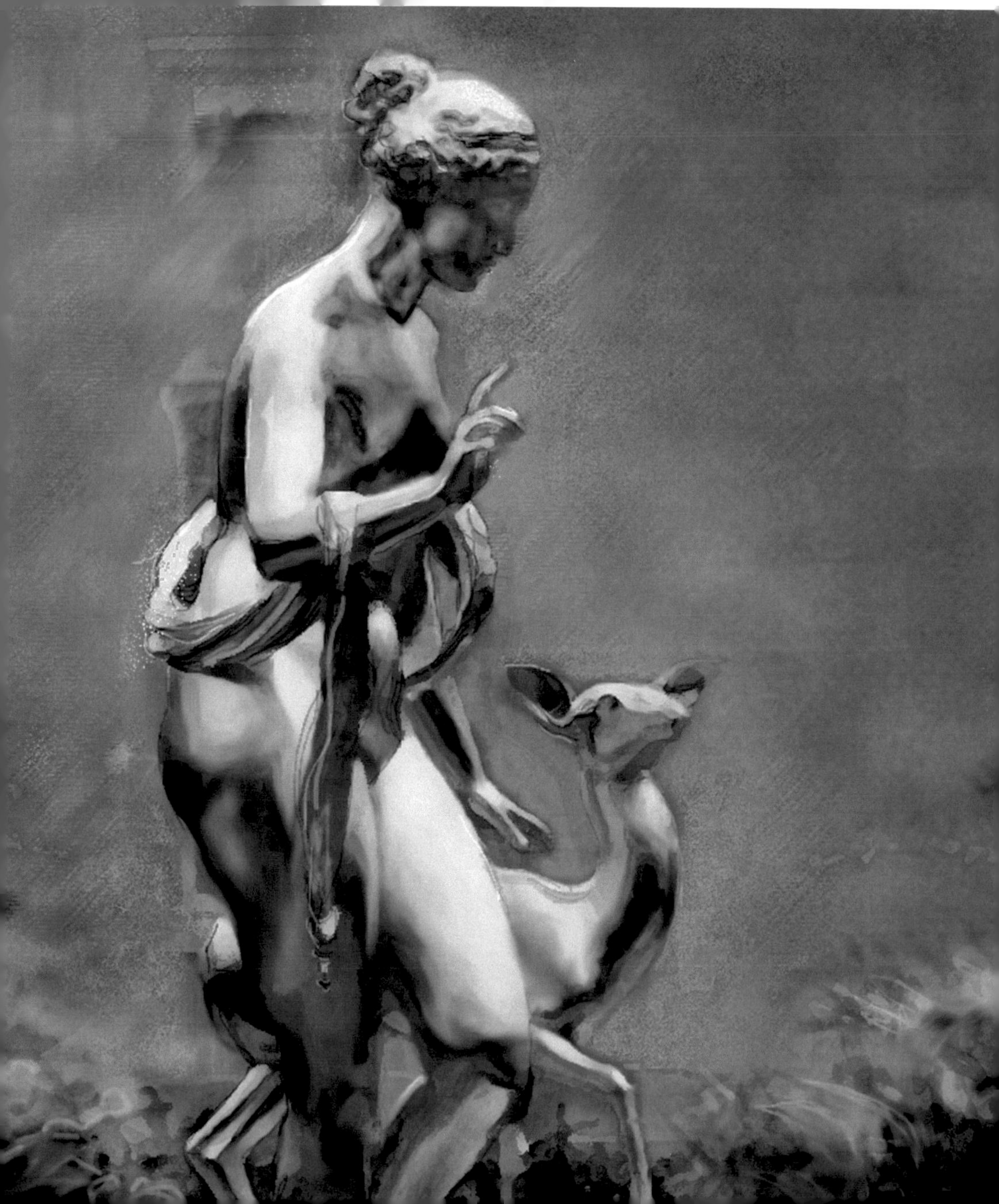

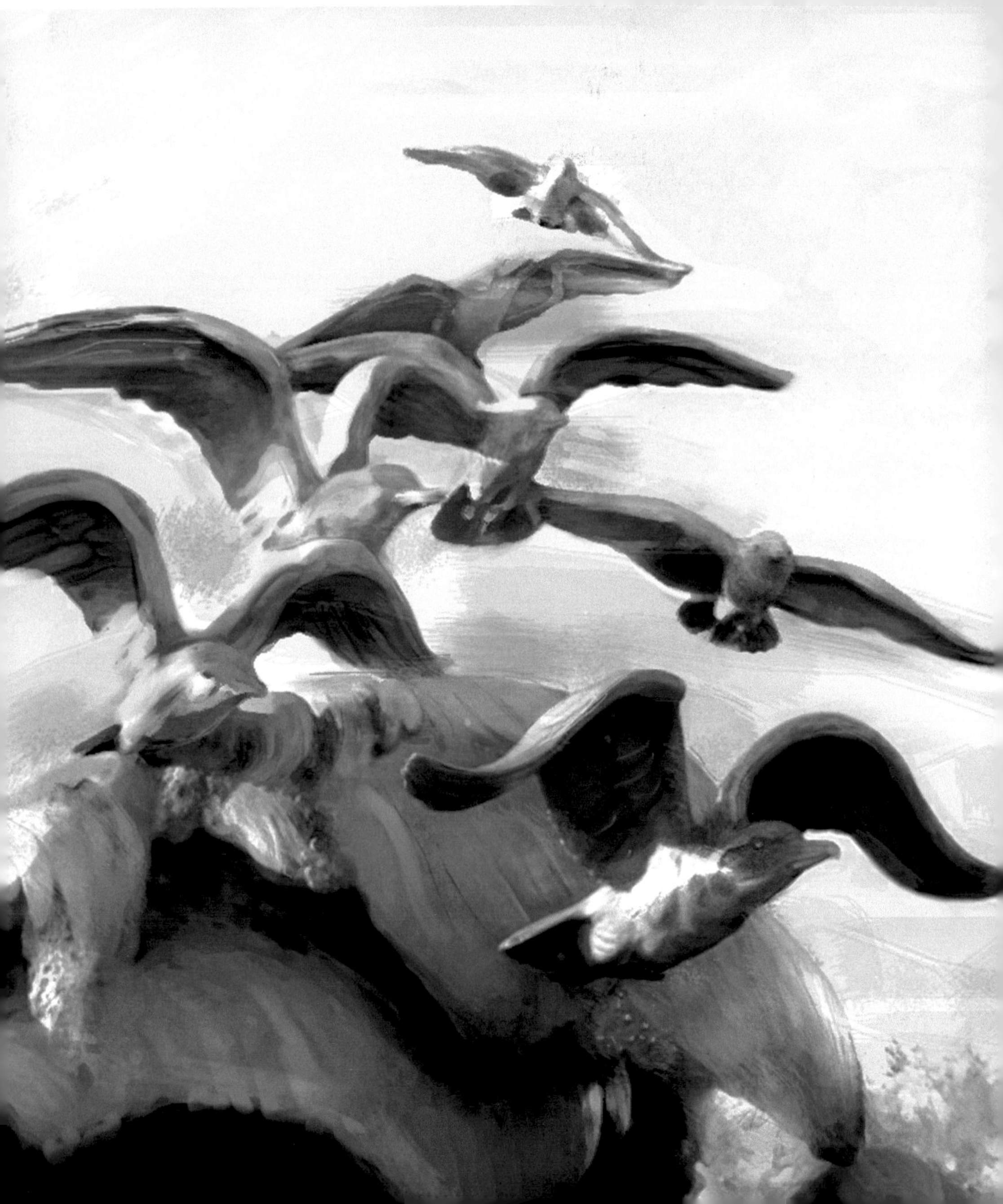

Gulls

Wing-tip to wing-tip
gulls hover over waves breaking
beside the Potomac.

O sailors and mariners
lost at sea, you know
how delicate is

the balance
between the next world
and this.

Gull

Gulls, sturdy, medium-sized seabirds with long pointed wings, a stout, hooked bill and webbed feet, are omnivorous scavengers and predators.

The constant companions of ships at sea, they are an appropriate image for the 1934 Navy-Marine Memorial, dedicated to "those who have gone down to the sea in ships and have done business in great waters." The memorial was a collaborative effort between Harvey W. Corbett, an architect whose firm was instrumental in the design of Rockefeller Center in New York, and Ernesto Begni del Piatta, an Italian who had come to the US to study law but abandoned it for sculpture. To construct the memorial, del Piatta employed the ancient lost wax metalsmith process to produce a cast of the relatively new aluminum material that was then coated with pigment. Funds for the memorial were donated by schoolchildren, government workers, and the sculptor himself. A plaque on the memorial reads: *To the strong souls and ready valor of those men of the United States who in the Navy, merchant marine and other paths of Activity upon the waters of the world have given life or still offer it in the performance of heroic deeds, this monument is dedicated by a grateful people.*

Ernesto Begni del Piatta, *Navy-Marine Memorial*, 1934. Cast aluminum, painted with green and yellow pigment. Lady Bird Johnson Park, George Washington Parkway, southwest of 14th Street Bridge.

Hare

Barry Flanagan's *Thinker on a Rock* (1999) is a humorous reference to one of the world's most familiar sculptures, *The Thinker* (1880) by Auguste Rodin. Flanagan, born in North Wales in 1941, says that while working with clay in the late 1970s, the image of a hare appeared "unveiling" itself before him. Since then, his monumental bronze hares have been displayed around the world.

Barry Flanagan, *Thinker on a Rock*, 1997. Bronze. National Gallery of Art Sculpture Garden, Constitution Avenue and 7th Street, NW.

In many cultures, the long-legged, long-eared hare represents fertility; but in Native American and African American folklore, the hare is mainly a trickster figure who easily outwits larger, fiercer opponents. In tales such as *Br'er Rabbit*, the rabbit hero is a jack rabbit, not a true rabbit but a hare, descendant of the European hare first brought to the North American continent in the 1600s. Hares, which nest instead of burrowing and bear young able to take care of themselves from birth, convey a spirit of independence that may have appealed to Flanagan, whose art often teases conventional ideas.

Hare

Thinker on a rock,
long-legged, long-eared, inhuman

but so like human thinkers
resting head-in-hand – in-paw! –

contemplating the meaning
of the world, the meaning of meaning:

oh, those stone abstractions
philosophers and statues

are so expert at, looking down upon
mere mortals walking in the garden here

singly, or in groups or pairs,
hiding, weaving or revealing

great and small affairs of state
and heart – simply living takes such art! –

Or are you only contemplating air?

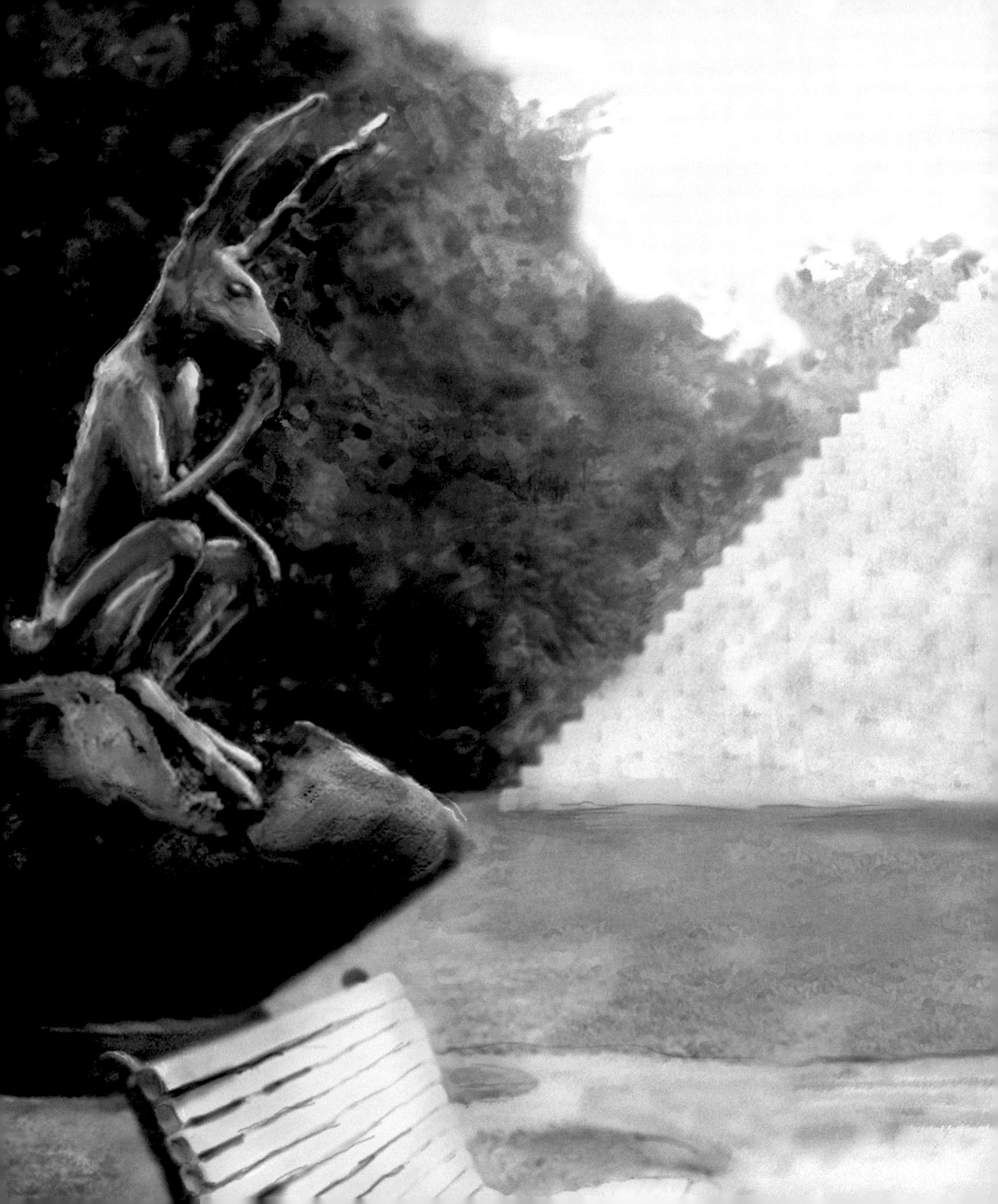

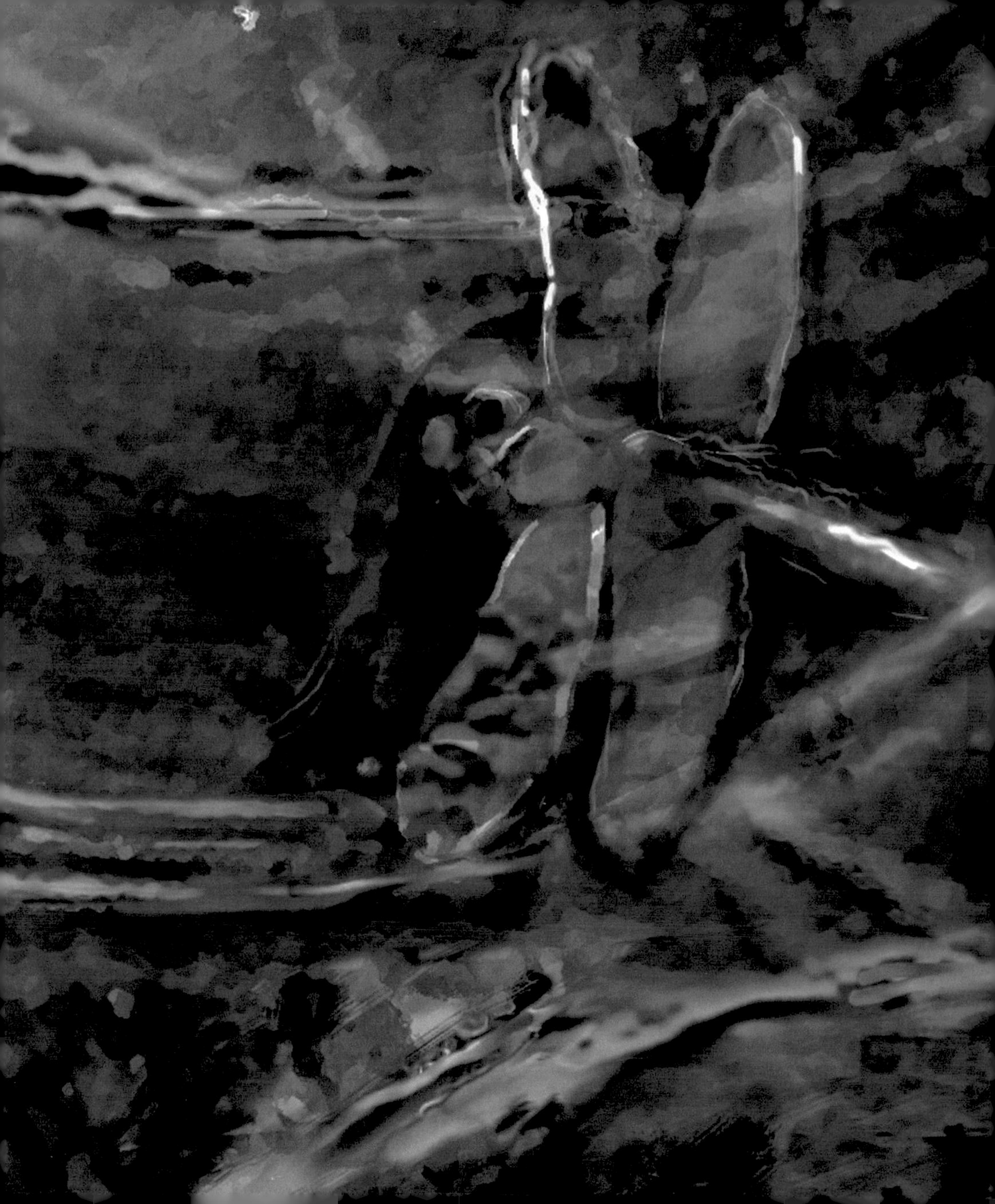

Insect

Blue-green shimmerer,
water-born skimmer

of brook and stream,
how you dart and hover,

jewelling the air, vibrating
filament wings to a high hum,

knotting legs into a net
to catch mosquitoes

as you fly!
O dragonfly,

O ceaseless-in-motion one,
at last you rest, bronze

on this bronze lily pad,
motionless.

Insect

David Phillips, *Lily Pond*, 1982. Bronze. John Marshall Park, C Street between 3rd and 4th Streets, NW.

Natural objects provide a recurring motif in the work of David Phillips, a 1970 graduate of the Cranbrook Academy of Art who often collaborates with landscape artists in his sculptures. Delicate bronze dragonflies, fish and frogs shimmer in the water of his *Lily Pond* in John Marshall Park. Designed by landscape architect Carol R. Johnson, the park commemorates the Chief Justice of the US Supreme Court whose 34 years on the bench from 1801-1835 established the foundations of American constitutional law. The Phillips fountain also commemorates the location of a spring from which water for public use was first piped through Washington's streets in 1808.

The dragonfly, which has existed for millions of years, as evidenced by 250 million-year-old fossil dragonflies, thrives in water environments. Aptly nicknamed "mosquitohawk," the dragonfly preys on smaller insects, snatching its prey from the air with legs arranged in a basket-like net. Flying at speeds up to 30 mph, its multifaceted, compound eyes can look in all directions at once. The absence of dragonfly nymphs, which live on fish and frogs as well as insects, is one of the signs of declining water quality.

Mrs. H. P. Whitney and the Enfield Pottery, Jaguar heads, adapted from Aztec and Mayan figures, ca. 1906. Painted terra-cotta. Art Museum of the Americas, 201 18th Street, NW, in the open fencing above the Flower Pool in the Aztec Garden.

Jaguar

The Spanish-colonial style Art Museum of the Americas, designed in the early 1900s by architects Paul Philippe Cret and Albert Kelsey, features an interior tile loggia, an open-air patio and the Blue Aztec Garden. The richly-colored tiles of the loggia and patio, manufactured at the Enfield Pottery in Pennsylvania, were modeled on Aztec and Inca characters. An open-work ceramic wall of jaguar-face masks borders the patio above a pool presided over by Xochipili, God of Flowers.

The jaguar, the largest member of the cat family in America, used to roam widely throughout the Americas. A ferocious swimmer, climber and runner, it is a symbol of strength and power in Aztec legend.

Jaguar

Jaguar, feared
and worshipped
as a god once,
still warrior-like,
helmet-clad

though stilled in stone,
how you rage
above the pool
of feathered serpents
and water-spouting frogs

at steel-framed mustangs
racing the asphalt paths
beyond this garden wall
heedless of monuments
to the past.

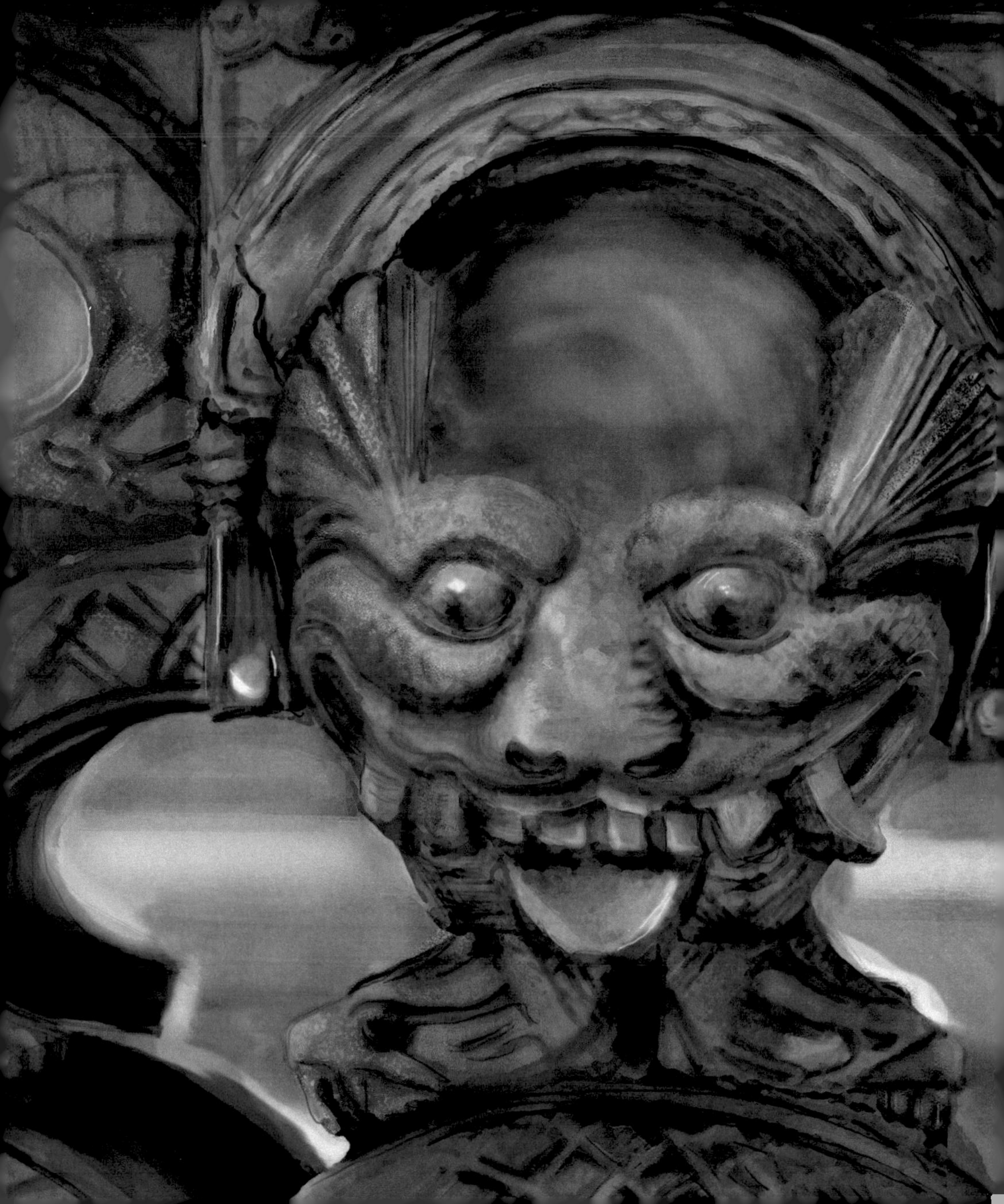

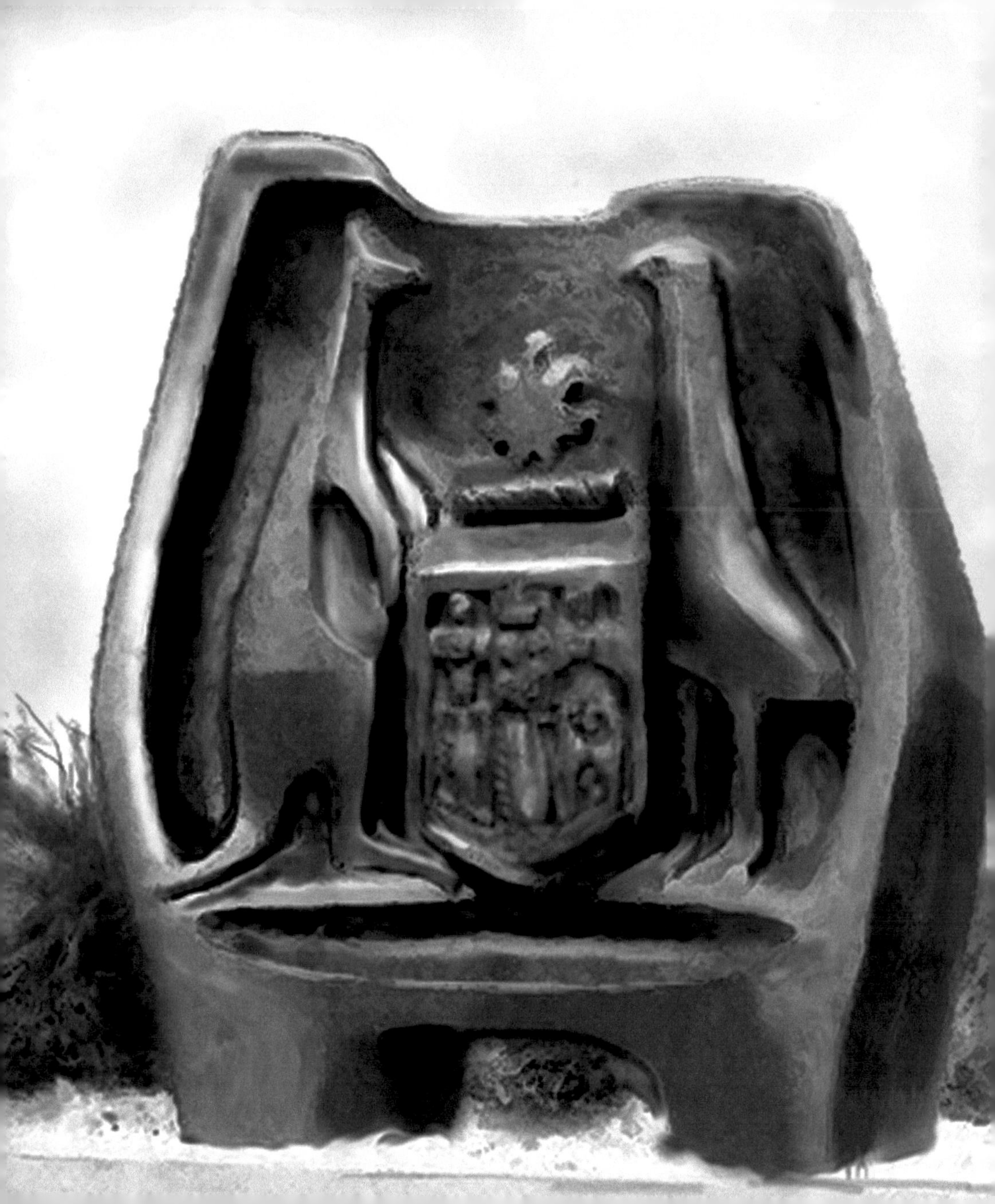

Kangaroo

The marsupial kangaroo,
joey in pouch,
bounds across
the Australian main.
Tame, at ease
in its vast forest range,
when hunted,
trapped, at bay,
it slashes out,
dangerous.

Far away
though at home
beside the embassy door
a kangaroo
and friendly emu
welcome visitor
and countryman.
Silent, composed
they gaze
upon their limits.

Kangaroo

Tom Bass, one of Australia's leading sculptors whose public artworks are on display in Sydney, Melbourne and Canberra, created this bronze *Australian Seal* (1969) that stands outside the Australian Embassy. The most prominent features on the coat of arms are the kangaroo, Australia's unofficial national animal, and the emu, another familiar image of Australian wildlife.

Thomas Bass, *Australian Seal*, 1969. Bronze. Australian Embassy, 1601 Massachusetts Avenue, NW.

A marsupial or "pouched" mammal, the kangaroo carries its joey in an external pocket. Native to Australia and New Guinea, the kangaroo has a small deer-like head, a long thick tail for balance, and large powerful hind legs that enable it to leap 25 feet and run 30 mph. When attacked, it kicks savagely with its hind legs.

Lion

The lion lives in prides, or family groups, in which females do the hunting and males maintain borders. When they reach maturity, males are expelled from the pride. Although known popularly as "king of the jungle," the lion is mainly found in the open plains of nature preserves in Africa where it is protected as a threatened species. An Asiatic subspecies once ranged from Greece to India through Persia; extinct in Greece by 100 C.E., this

Anonymous, *Canova Lions*, ca. 1869, after Italian originals by Antonio Canova, 1792. Bronze. Corcoran Gallery of Art, 17th Street & New York Avenue, NW.

group survived in the Middle East and North Africa until the 20th century, but now only a small group inhabits a sanctuary in India.

The lion has been given more attention in art and literature than any other animal as a symbol of power and authority. It has long played a role in architectural decoration as well. The two massive bronze lions on the Corcoran Gallery steps, for example, were cast from a mold made from the marble lions of the Italian neoclassical sculptor Antonio Canova (1757-1822) that decorate the cenotaph of Pope Clement XIII in St. Peter's in Rome. These bronze "Canova lions" were brought to the US by millionaire Benjamin Holladay (1819-1887) who made his fortune transporting pioneers from St. Louis to California on the Holladay Overland Stagecoach. William Wilson Corcoran, a banker, investor and, as founder of the Corcoran Gallery of Art, Washington's first great philanthropist, purchased the lions in 1888; and in 1897, when the Corcoran moved into the Ernest Flagg's Renaissance Revival building on 17th Street, NW, he placed them beside the entrance. Although the bronze lions recline at their ease, one awake and one half asleep, they retain a muscular might and regal presence.

Lion

How lazily the lions lie,
heads on paws,
flanking the entrance
to the Beaux-Arts museum.
Across the Ellipse,
a glimpse of the White House;
inside these great halls,
the peace of heart
that comes with meditating
on art.

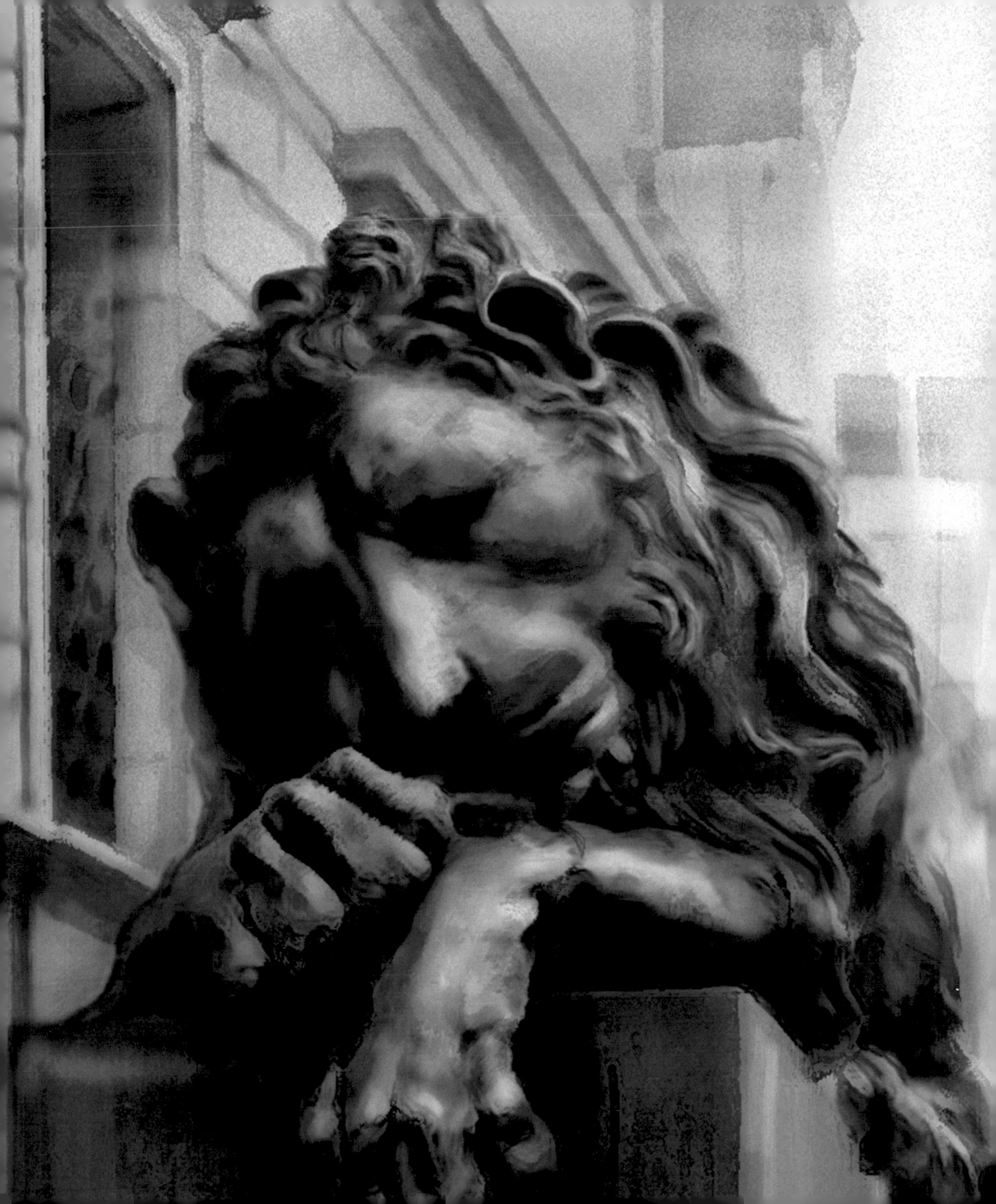

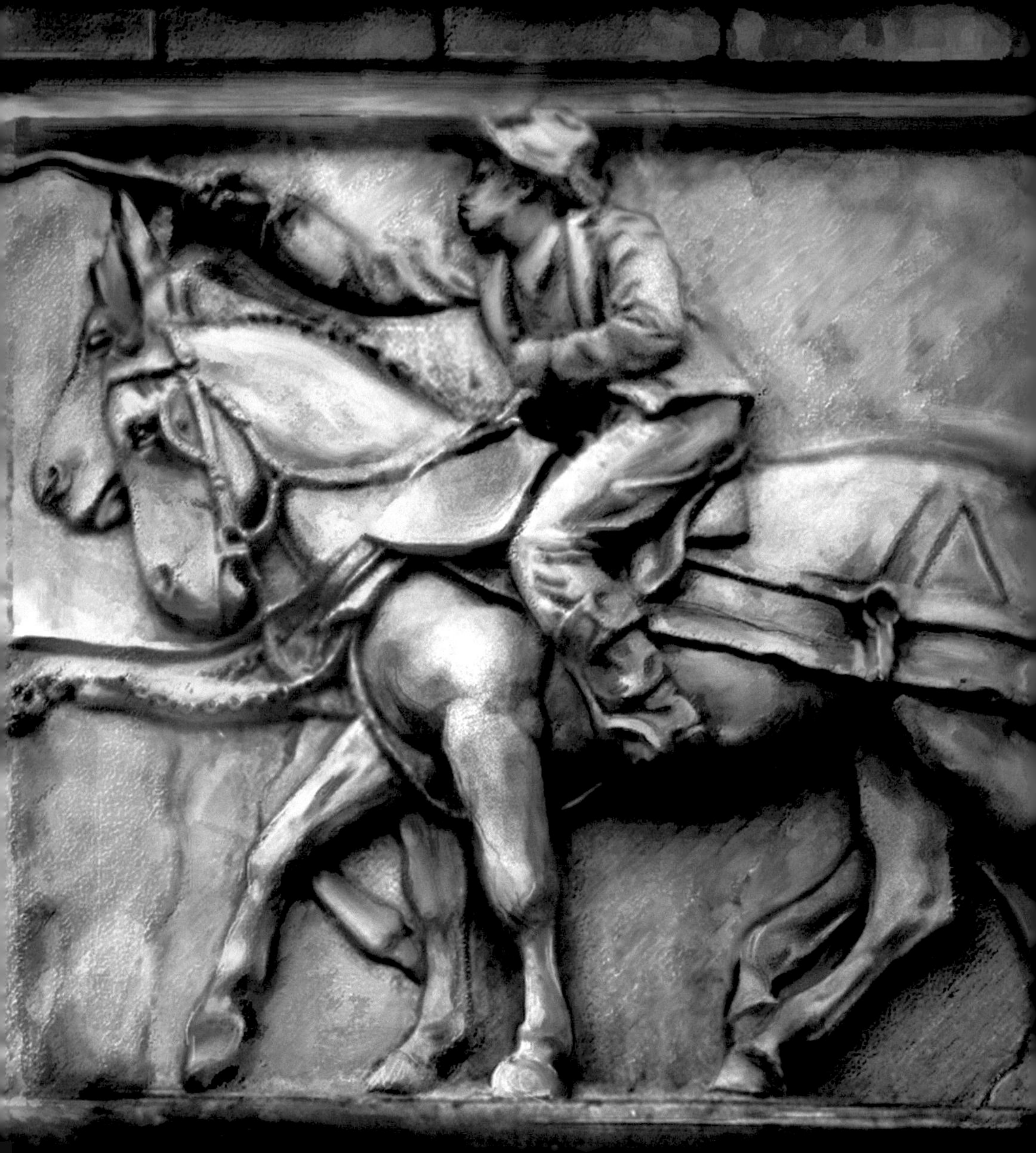

Mule

Officers on excitable stallions shout orders
to the ranks of soldiers –
grizzle-bearded men
and smooth-faced boys, rifles
over shoulders, some conversing,
some glancing backwards,
most wordlessly trudging –

while the wounded (blinded,
bandaged, stumbling
on crutches) limp forward
leaning against the less-injured,

and the supply wagon
pulled by mules (that sturdy,
dependable, personable crossbreed
of horse and donkey)
takes up the rear of this file
of Union veterans marching
through the Capital
in eternal terra-cotta formation.

Mule

General Montgomery Meigs (1816-1892), Lincoln's Quartermaster General during the Civil War, designed the brick and iron Pension Building in 1882 for the purpose of dispensing pensions to veterans. After touring the building, General Philip Sheridan was rumored to have said it had only one problem: "It's fireproof." Modeled in part after the 16th century Palazzo Farnese in Rome with a vast interior courtyard and external frieze, it is one of the jewels of Washington architecture. Running around the outside between the first and second floors is a dramatic terra-cotta frieze designed by Carl Buberl (1834-1899). A 1954 emigrant from Bohemia (now the Czech Republic), Buberl became a prominent sculptor of Civil War memorials, including the Soldiers and Sailors Memorial Arch in Hartford, Connecticut, perhaps the first triumphal arch in the US. The *Quartermaster Panel*, one of seven different panel designs of the Pension Building frieze, depicts a mule and an African-American driver, or muleskinner, regulars of the Quartermaster or Supply Corps.

The mule, a sterile cross between a mare (or female horse) and a jack (or male donkey) has been used for hundreds of years as a draft and pack animal. George Washington, who felt horses "ate too much, worked too little, and died too young," is thought to have been the first mule breeder in the US. Since the late 19th century, the mule has been the official mascot of the US Army.

Casper Buberl, *Quartermaster Panel*, based in part on Parthenon designs, 1882. Terra-cotta frieze circling the facade of the National Building Museum (former Pension Building), 5th and F Streets, NW.

Timothy Parker

Newt

Newt is the name commonly used for a number of small amphibians having elongated bodies, flattened tails, and two pairs of limbs which can be regenerated when lost. Inhabiting small streams and moist places in woods, the carnivorous newt feeds on insects and other small animals.

Steven Weitzman, *Centennial Tree*, 1990. Willow oak trunk. Formerly at National Zoo.

Sculptor Steven Weitzman carved more than 50 images, from spiders and amphibians to humans, from a single willow oak trunk in 1988-90. He carved the sculpture on location and attracted crowds who watched its progress. Dedicated to the zoo volunteers, the sculpture, which originally stood across from the Education Building, has been removed due to disintegration.

Newt

From a willow oak trunk
the artist has carved
a sculpture of us all:

human, bird, beast
and, by no means least,
amphibian –

this small salamander,
the flat-tailed newt, emerging
from its wooden vegetation –

a harmony
of legs and tails,
feathers and claws, all

so close together
it's hard to tell
where one ends

and another begins.

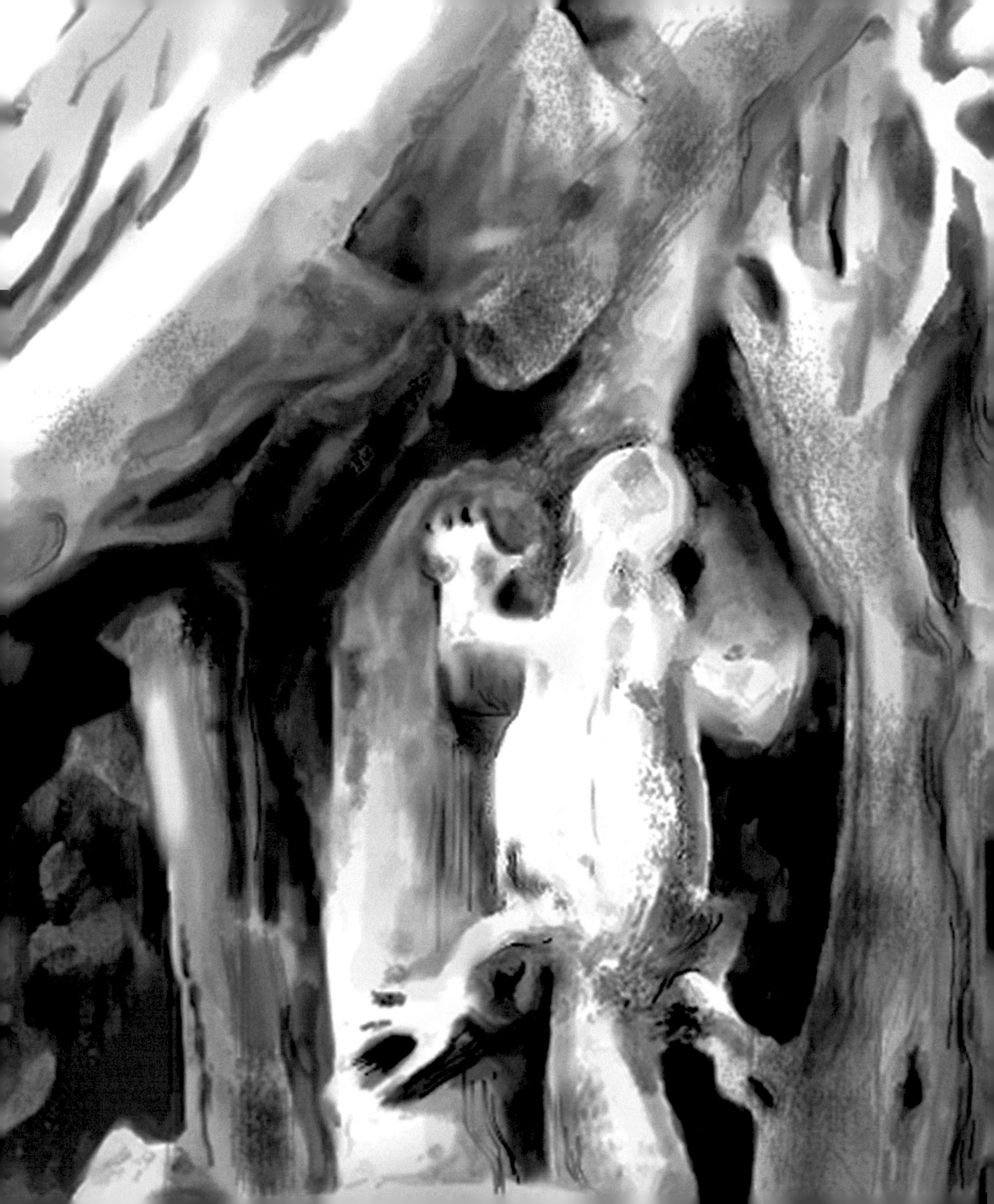

Owl

Emblem of wisdom
and observation
easily overlooked
among the city's grander
marble monuments,
more durable bronzes,
the copper owl
with companions
serpent and lynx
crests the eaves
of this academy
of science.

Lee Lawrie, *Wisdom and Observation*, 1923. Copper cresting. National Academy of Sciences, 2101 Constitution Avenue, NW.

Owl

A nocturnal raptor, or bird of prey, the owl has exceptional sight, an acute sense of hearing, and soft plumage that muffles the sound of flight – all aiding in the element of surprise in the owl's attacks on its prey. With its large head and forward-facing eyes, the owl has become a symbol of wisdom: in Indian lore, the owl represents insight and prophecy; in Greek myth, it is the sacred bird of Athena, goddess of wisdom.

This owl, part of a striking three-foot-high copper cresting of owls, lions and serpents atop the National Academy of Sciences building, was designed by Lee Lawrie (1877-1963), one of America's foremost architectural sculptors. Lawrie came from Germany as a child, and studied sculpture with Augustus Saint-Gaudens. In addition to architectural work at the Neoclassical National Academy of Sciences, his most significant works include architectural sculpture at the United States Military Academy, Yale University, Rockefeller Center and the state capital at Lincoln, Nebraska.

Penguin

The flightless swimming penguin, first documented by Vasco de Gama in 1497 along the coast of South Africa, lives in the wild solely in the Antarctic. This water-spouting penguin is one

Anonymous, *Hoff Memorial Fountain*, 1934. Concrete. Walter Reed Army Medical Center, Aspen Street between Georgia Avenue and 16th Street, NW.

of four concrete penguins of the *Hoff Memorial Fountain* at Walter Reed Army Medical Center, named for Army surgeon Walter Reed (1815-1902), a specialist in tropical medicine who discovered that the yellow fever virus is carried by mosquitoes. Rensselaer Hoff (1848-1920), an Army doctor who dramatically improved the organization and efficiency of the Medical Corps, was once stationed in the Arctic, which the penguin fountain may mistakenly represent. In 2003, the fountain was the site of a dramatic rescue of several ducklings which couldn't climb up the steep ledge of the pool. Walter Reed firefighters hosed in water to raise the level so that the ducklings could walk out of the fountain. For the next few days, until the ducks were strong enough to climb out at a lower water level, the fountain was kept filled to the brim.

Penguin

Four plump penguins
properly prim
on the fountain's
military rim
spout water into
the turquoise pool –
ah, it's cool! –
all summer,

while in low relief
on columns beneath
hooded cobras sway,
enchanting,
poison-fanged.

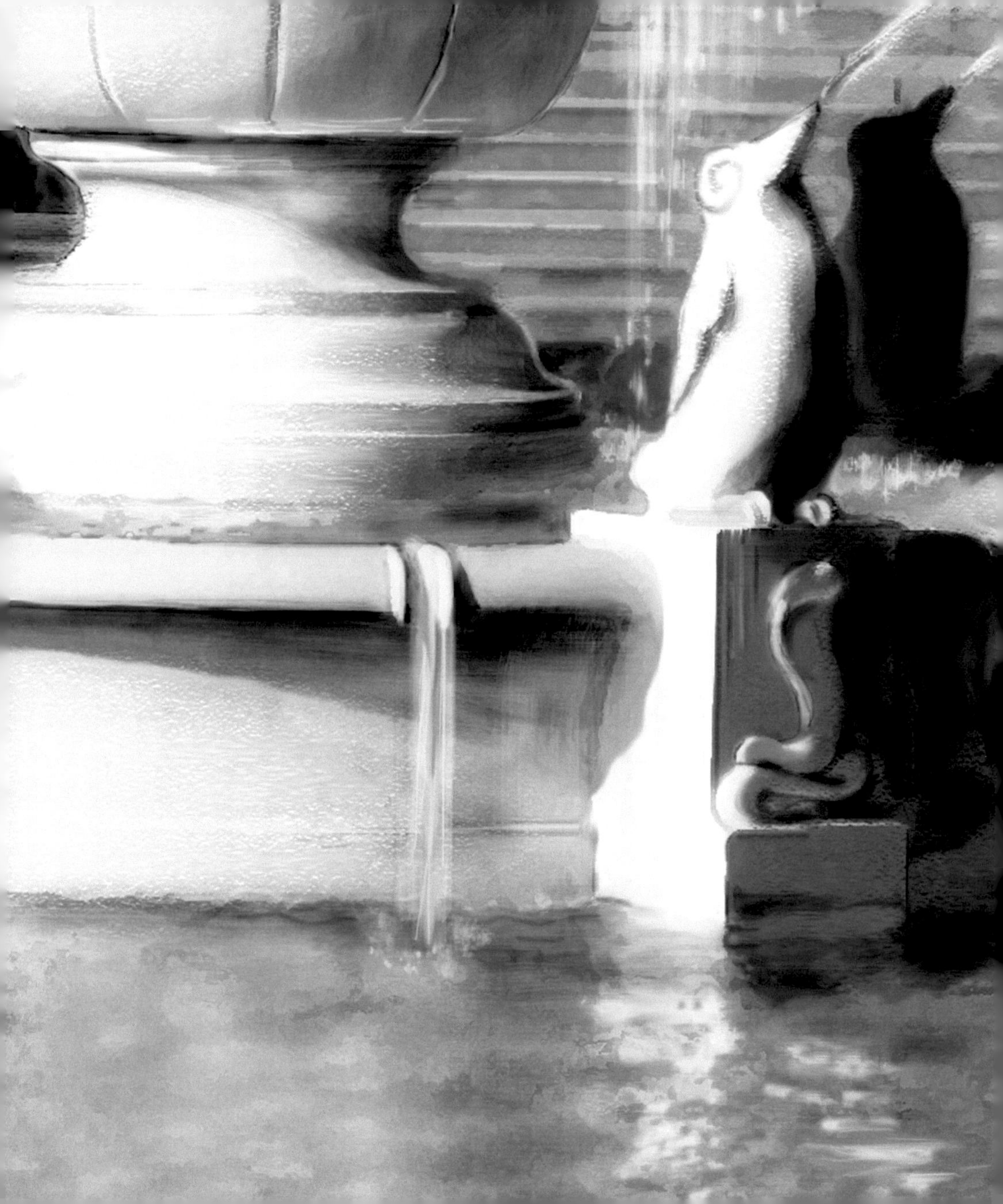

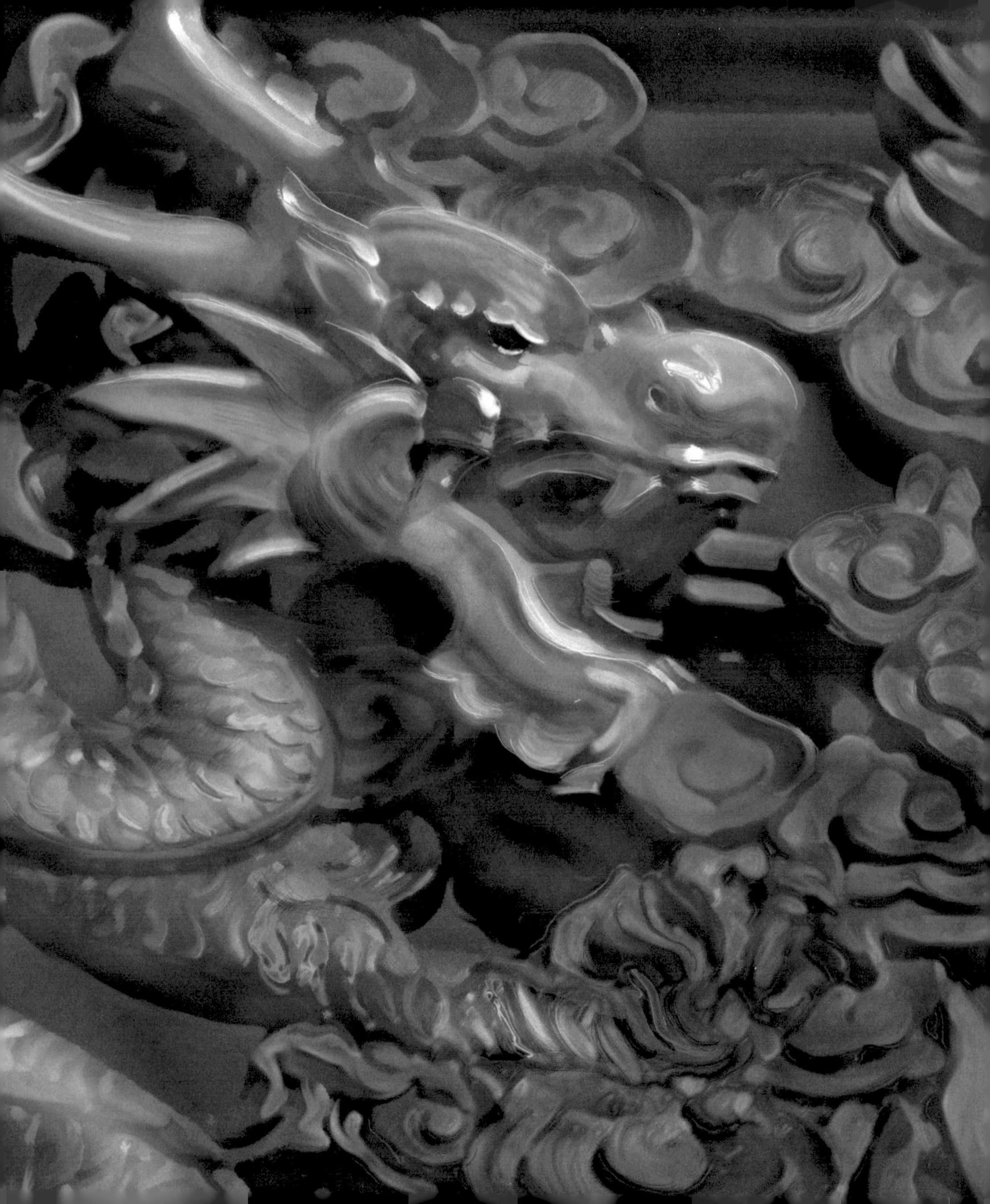

Qing Dynasty Dragon

Open-mouthed, tongues
aflame, gold dragons writhe
never quite intertwined,
two by two circling
each other throughout
eternity, yin and
yang, female and male,
creative and destructive,
ferociously whirling.

From where you stand
on the busy city walk
look up at the red and gold
gateway, through the
open-work dragon-panels
into the sky. See
how the dragons move –
advance, retreat, turn,
counterturn from whatever
came before. Then step
beneath the arch to the other
side, as though to another shore.

Qing Dynasty Dragon

In Chinese lore, the dragon, one of the twelve symbols of sovereignty, represents the natural world, adaptability and transformation. Two dragons placed together but facing away from each other form the symbol for Yin and Yang, the female and male principles, the two fundamental forces of the universe.

Alfred Liu, *Friendship Arch*, 1986. Painted wood and ceramic tile. Spanning H Street at 7th Street, NW.

Dragons are a recurring sculptural motif in Chinatown's majestic Welcome Gate or Friendship Arch, the world's largest single-span Chinese arch, a joint project of the governments of Washington, DC, and Beijing. Architect Alfred Liu designed the arch based on the symbolism of celebration from the Ming-Qing dynasties. The colorful red, green, blue and gold seven-roof wooden structure contains 7,000 tile and 272 painted dragons.

River Horse

The barrel-shaped, stumpy-legged hippopotamus (Greek for "river horse") is a member of the even-toed ruminant ungulate mammals, a group that includes deer, cows, sheep and antelope. New genetic evidence also suggests that hippos share a common ancestor with dolphins, whales and porpoises: like cetaceans, hippos lack hair and are capable of vocalizing underwater. Hippos live in the wild only in Africa where they spend the day relaxing in the water and the nights grazing on land.

Anonymous, GW Hippopotamus, unknown date. Bronze. George Washington University, near Lisner Auditorium, 21st and I Streets, NW.

According to a legend cited by George Washington University President Stephen Trachtenburg, who found this bronze sculpture in an antique shop in 1996 and donated it to the school, George and Martha Washington used to watch hippos rise from the shallow waters of the Potomac River near their home at Mount Vernon where children would try to stroke them. Now the hippo is the university's unofficial mascot; students rub the bronze hippo's nose and toss coins in his mouth, which the homeless then collect. A verse on the plaque highlights the good feelings people have about hippos:

>*Art for wisdom*
>*Science for joy*
>*Politics for beauty*
>*And a Hippo for hope*

River Horse

Out of the Potomac shallows
the hippopotamus rose –
so legend goes –
and George and Martha from their porch
at Mount Vernon tried to lure it
onto the grass.

A hippo for hope
young scholars intone,
rubbing its nose
to gold for good luck,
tossing coins into its mouth
as they pass
which the homeless retrieve
to clink against the cold.

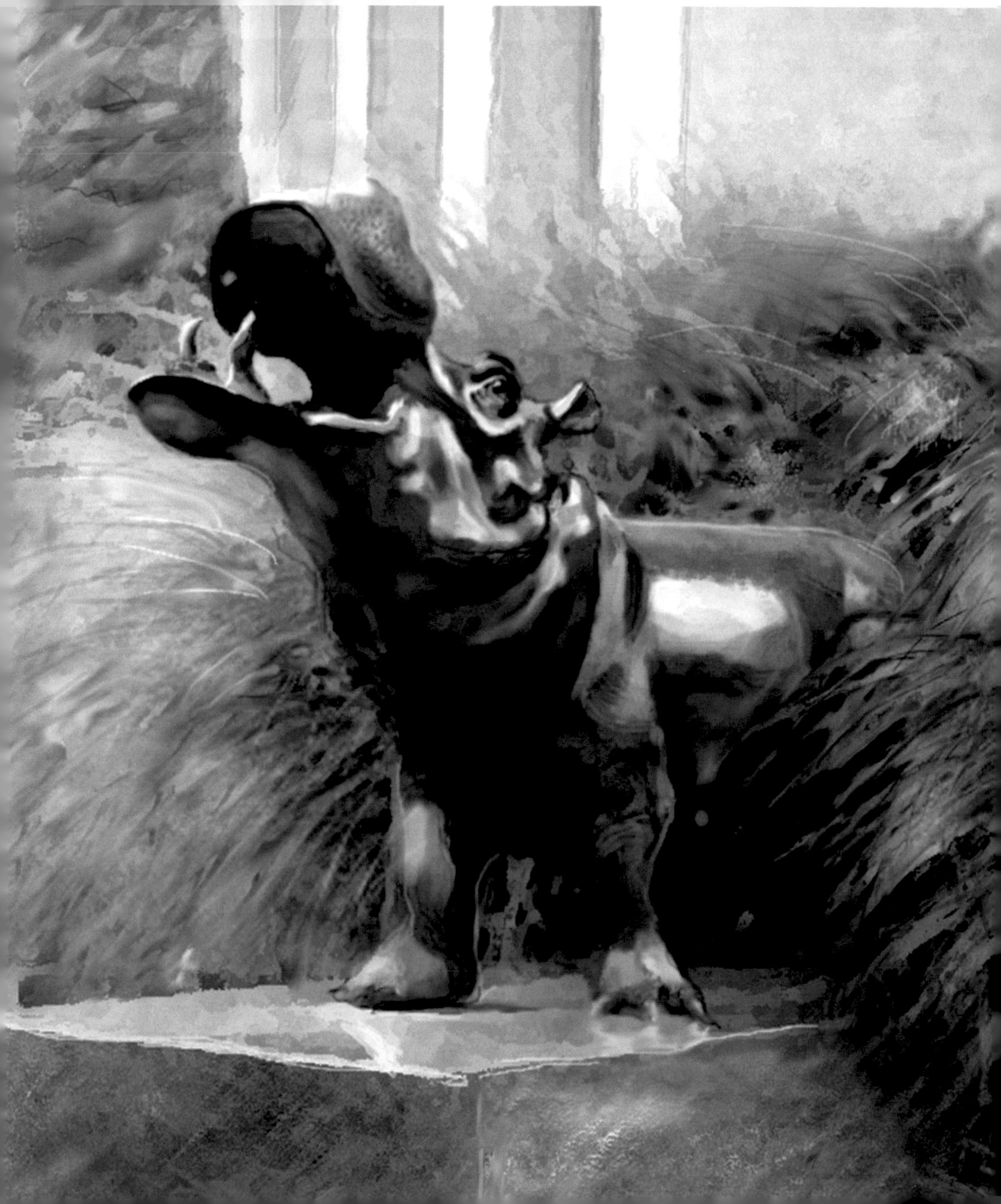

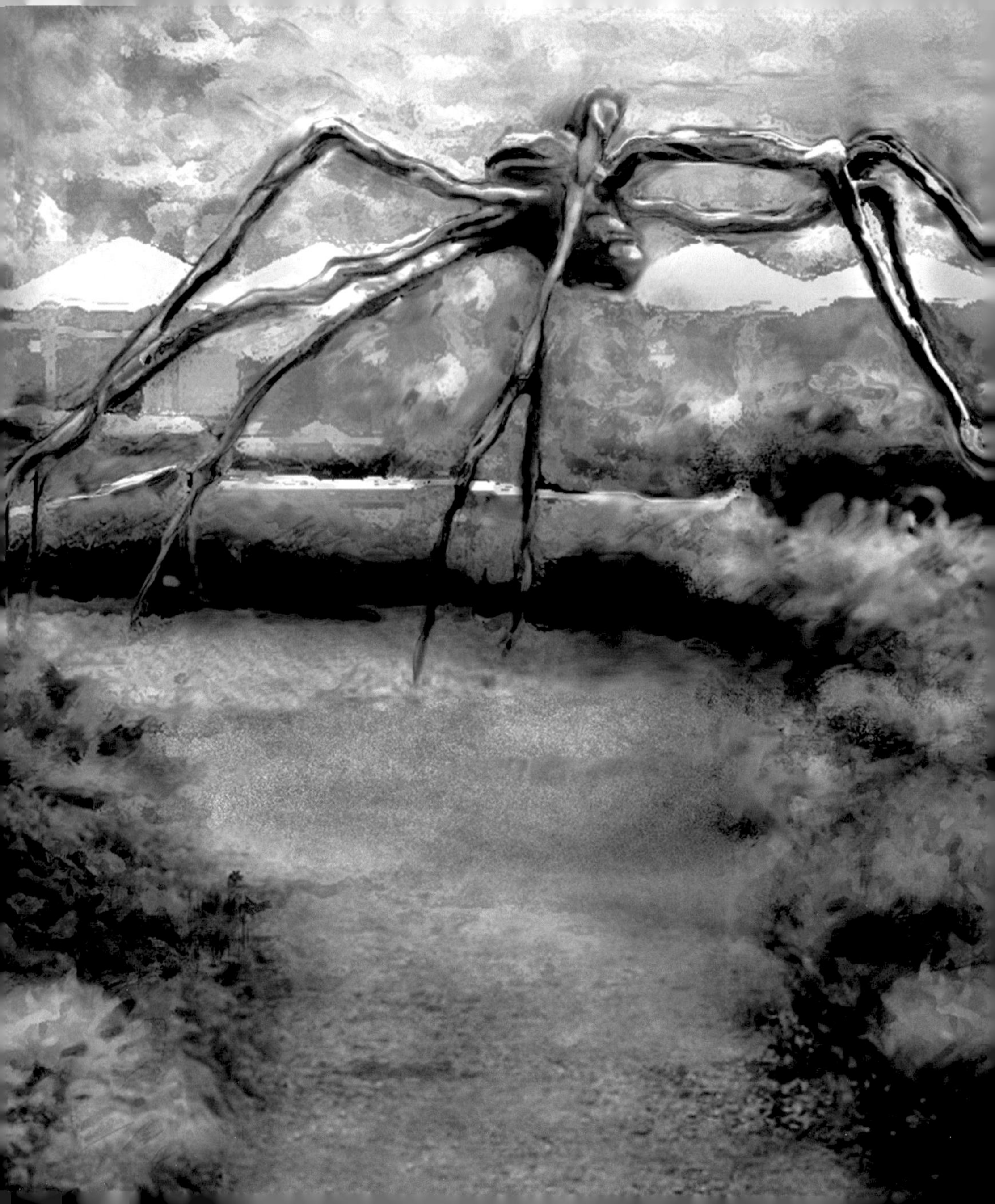

Spider

To round the path in the garden
and confront
the spider looming,
leering, menacingly striding,
is to be, as by a small fear magnified,
thrust aside from the self,
panting, flushed.

But to crawl beneath
the great maternal body
and into the cave of legs
powerful, delicate, silver-patinaed,
is to become a child again,
protected, safe
in the mother's arms,
invulnerable to harm,
to all tempest-toss

but the sting of childhood lost.

Louise Bourgeois, *Spider*, 1996. Bronze. National Gallery of Art Sculpture Garden, Constitution Avenue at 7th Street, NW.

Timothy Parker

Spider

Arachnids, a class which also includes scorpions, ticks and mites, were among the first animals to live on land, about 400-500 million years ago. Spiders, like other arthropods, have a hard exoskeleton and four pairs of jointed appendages: the first pair, pincers or fangs; the second pair, pincers or feelers for holding or killing prey; and two pairs used as legs for walking. Spiders are solitary except when mating or guarding their young. They contribute to the balance of nature by controlling populations of insects and their plant or animal hosts.

For sculptor Louise Bourgeois, the spider is a protective, maternal figure she relates to her own mother. Bourgeois (b. 1911 in Paris), studied at the École du Louvre and the Académie des Beaux-Arts. She worked first in Paris as a graphic artist and engraver; then, after moving to New York in 1938, she began to design sculptural pieces, first abstract wooden shapes, then larger pieces in bronze, rubber and stone. Her childhood, which for her "has never lost its magic, never lost its mystery, never lost its drama," is a dominant theme. Since the 1980s, Bourgeois has been developing a body of work, from drawings to large-scale sculptures, with the spider as the central figure. Her large bronze *Spider* (1996) set in the National Gallery of Art Sculpture Garden, is both formidable and comforting; another, in a very different atmosphere in Tokyo, is more cartoonish. For Bourgeois, "Art guarantees sanity," and the transformation of materials into art, she asserts, is "like the conversion of electricity into power."

Turtle

Herman Atkins MacNeil, Turtle lamps. Bronze. Plaza of the United States Supreme Court, 1 First Street, NE.

Turtle, the generic name for the reptiles that include terrapins and tortoises, is an air-breathing reptile whose body is protected by a bony shell. In size, turtles range from a few inches to about six feet. Long-lived, with some individuals more than 150 years old, the turtle has existed since the era of the dinosaurs, 200 million years ago.

This bronze turtle, one of many symbolic architectural elements at the United States Supreme Court sculpted by Herman Atkins MacNeil (1866-1947), functions as a base for a light fixture on the plaza. Two larger allegorical figures flanking the steps leading up to the courthouse represent Justice and Mercy. The building itself was designed in 1932 by Gilbert Cass (1859-1934) known as "The Skyscraper Pioneer" for his Woolworth Building in New York City. For the design of the Supreme Court, Gilbert employed a neoclassical structure to emphasize the ideals of order and democracy. The turtle, long equated with determination and persistence, suggests that justice may be slow, but will prevail.

Turtle

High on the high court's
stone facade somber letters promise all
Equal Justice Under Law.

Two figures in flowing marble robes
enthroned beside the steps below
contemplate mercy and the authority of rule.

A small bronze turtle hidden
in a corner, thrusting out neck,
gripping with legs and claws,

strains forward under the weight
of a lamp that illuminates
the slow but steady progress of justice.

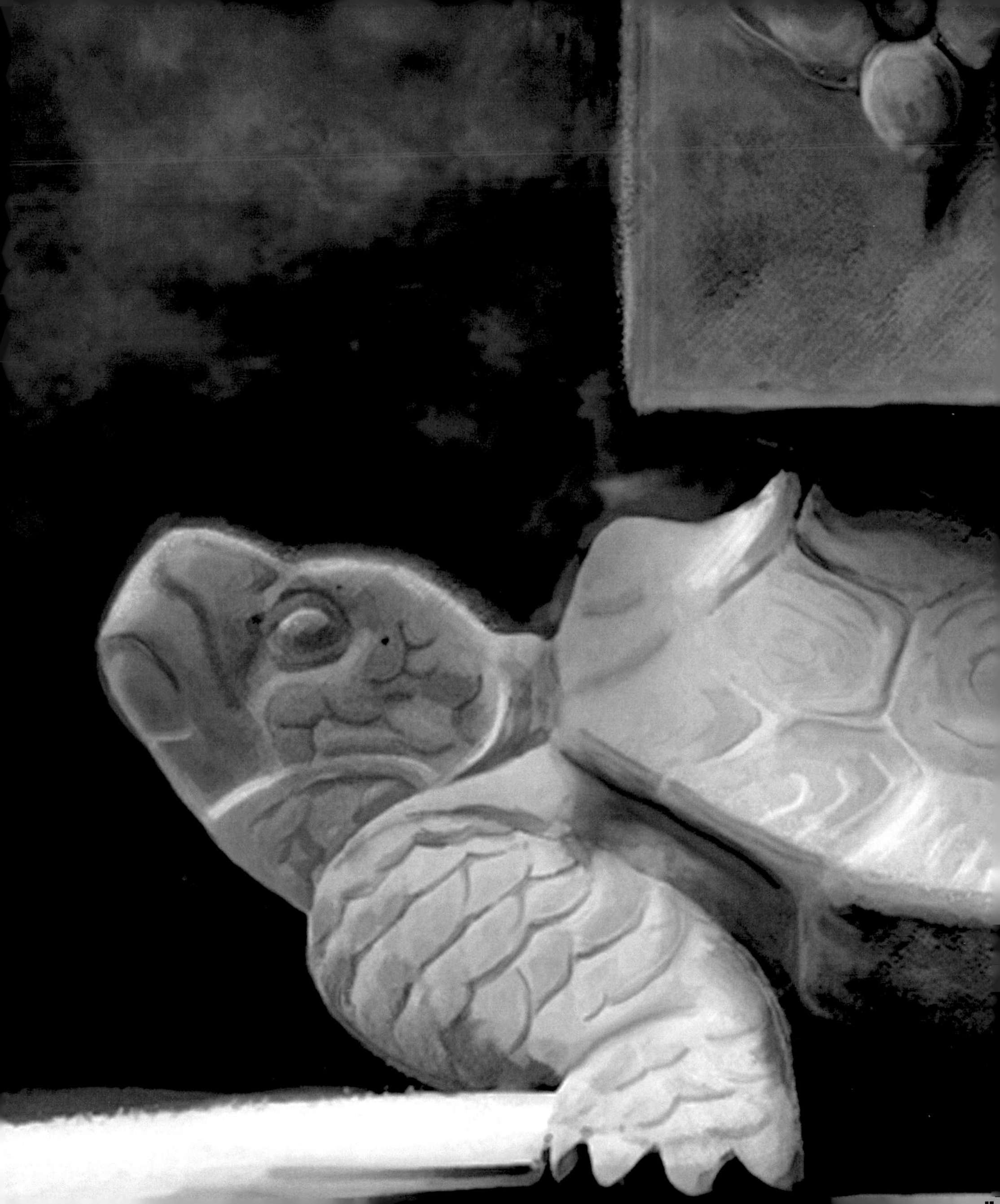

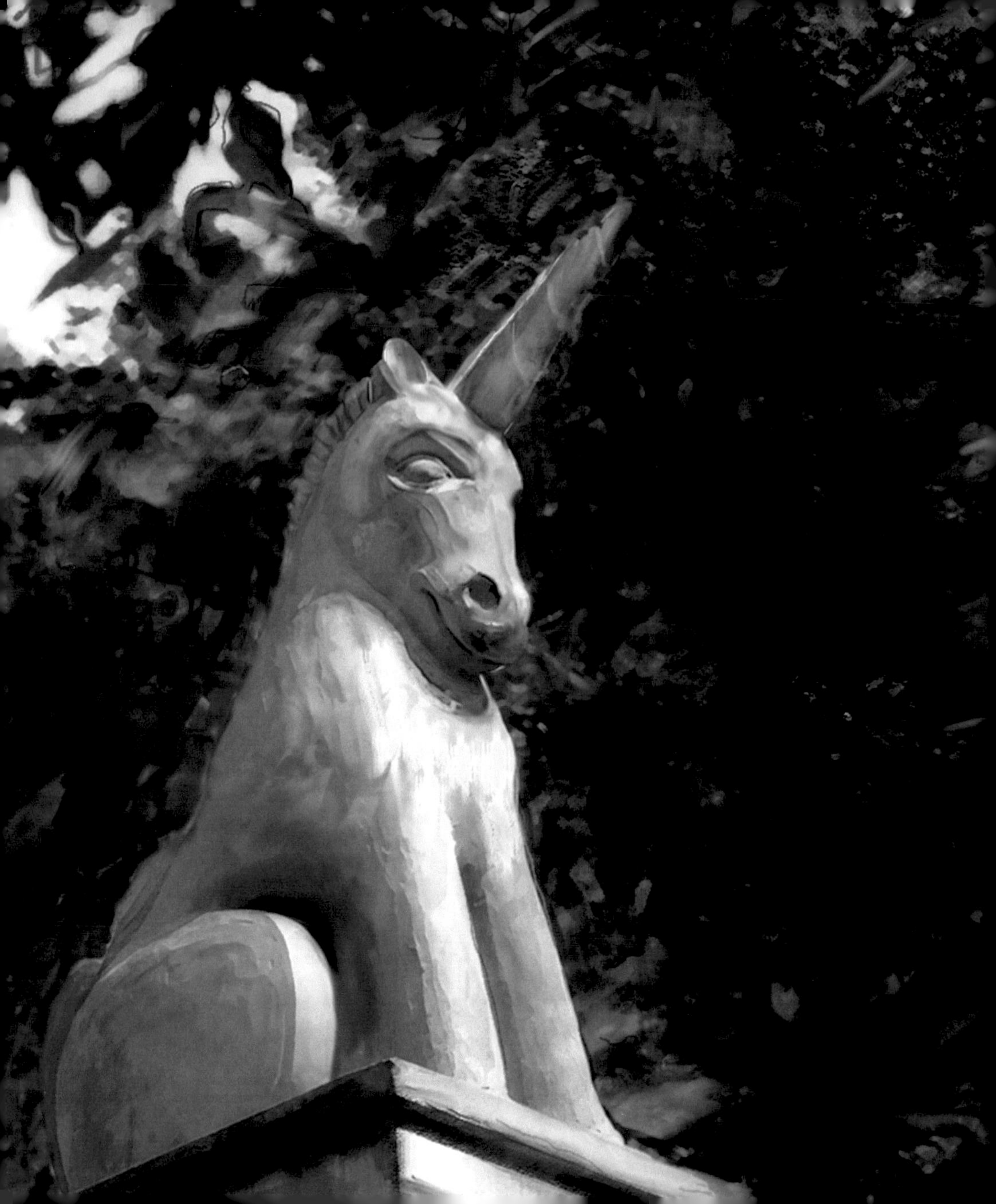

Unicorn

Royal horse
with single horn
(symbol of purity
in ancient tapestries),
the unicorn stares deep
into woods,
wishing to leap far
from this city lane
it names and guards.

Unicorn

Anonymous, *Unicorns*, ca. 1970. Cast concrete (?). Unicorn Lane at Oregon Avenue, NW.

Two large unicorns appearing to be of cast concrete overlook Rock Creek Park at Unicorn Lane in upper NW. The name comes from the Latin *onus* for "one" and *cornus* for "horn." In medieval legend, the horn of this gentle, magical creature was sought as an antidote to poison. But shy, selfless and solitary, the unicorn could be tamed only by the purest young maidens. Medieval European travelers who returned from Africa with descriptions of the one-horned rhinoceros may have inspired the tales of the unicorn.

Vietnamese Ox

Jeanne Gavaert, *Kouprey*, 1967. Bronze bas relief. Education Building foyer, east wall. National Zoo.

One of the world's rarest animals, now critically endangered, the kouprey has become the prime symbol of conservation efforts in Indochina. A grass-eating forest ox of the low, rolling hills of Vietnam, Cambodia, Thailand and Laos, it lives in small herds of up to twenty members. Both males and females sport branching antlers. Mysterious, elusive, and one of the least known of all large mammals, the kouprey may be one of the most important genetically because of its resistance to disease and its tropical fortitude. Westerners first observed a kouprey at the zoo in Paris in 1937, which Dr. Harold Jefferson Coolidge correctly identified and described in 1940. After this kouprey died of starvation during the Nazi occupation, little new information about the species was discovered until 1957, when biologist Charles Wharton conducted his still-definitive field study. Subsequent fieldwork was interrupted by the war in Vietnam, and the last verified sightings occurred in 1988. Although scientists conducted another major search for the kouprey in 1994, only footprints were found, leading to fears of the kouprey's extinction. The bronze relief of this herd of kouprey, sculpted by Jeanne Gavaert in 1967, is dedicated to Dr. Coolidge.

Vietnamese Ox

A herd of wild ox
from Vietnam
gallops in bronze
across the wall.

Victim of war,
almost extinct,
the kouprey teaches this:
treasure what exists.

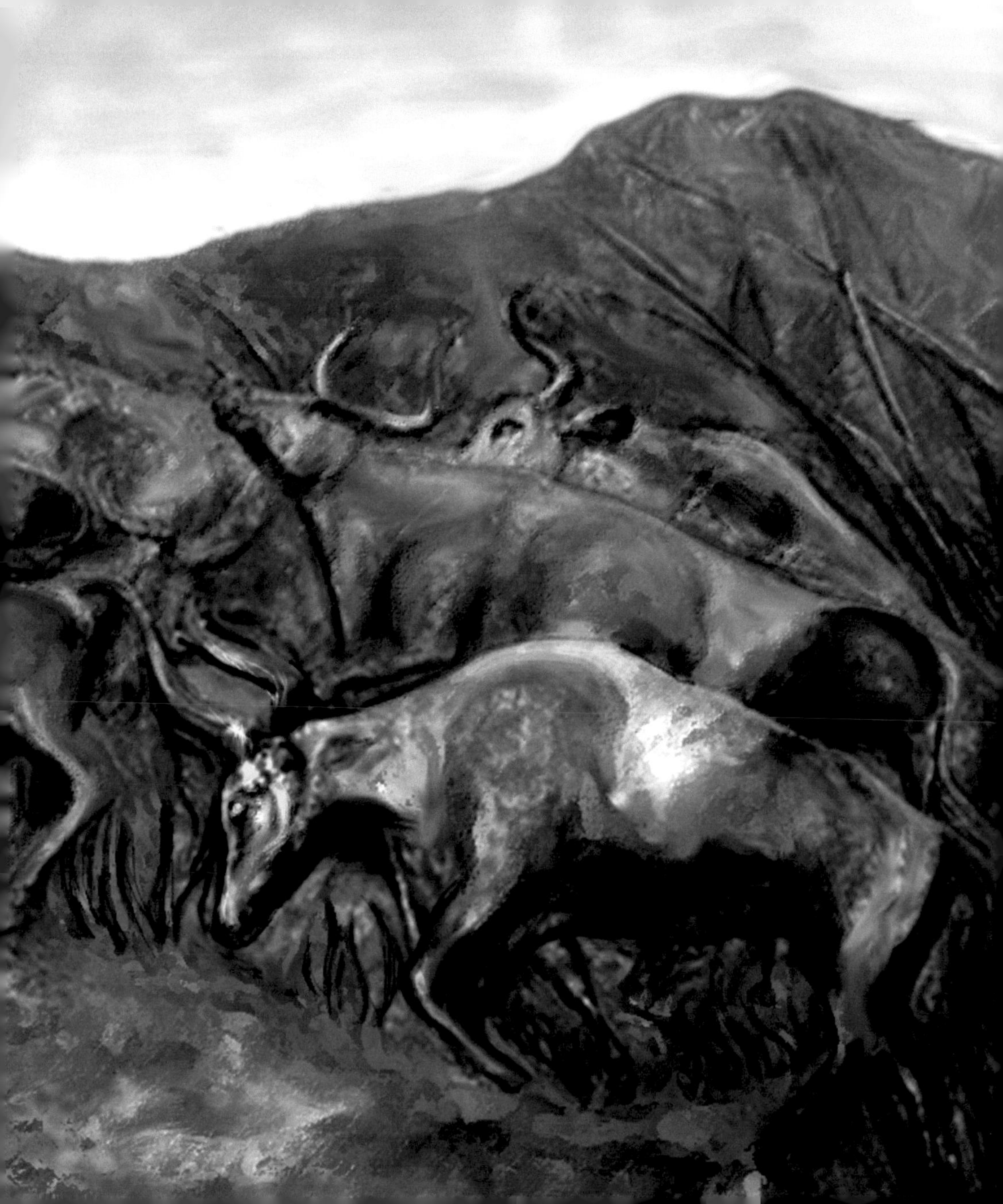

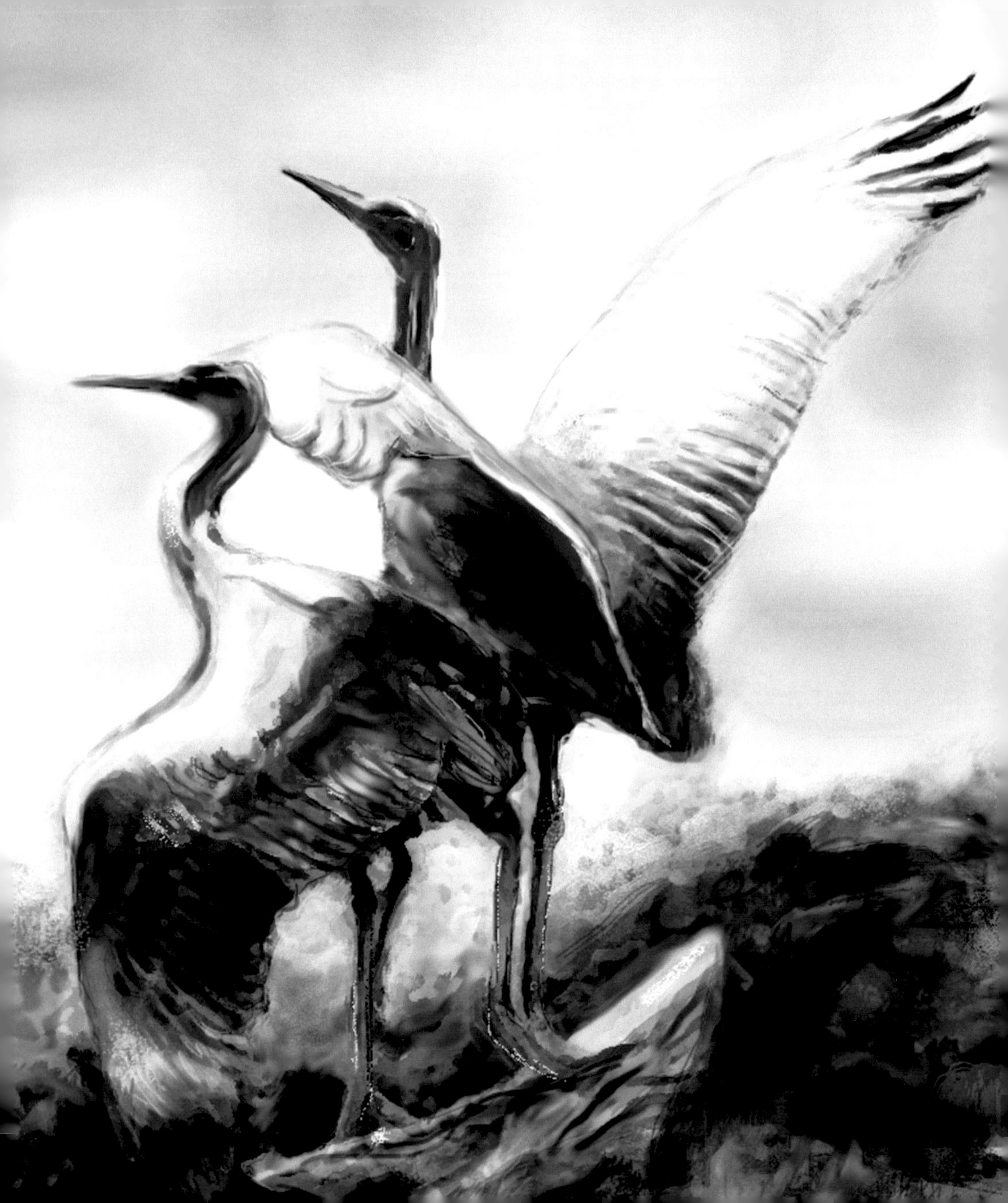

Whooping Crane

Grus Americanus,
heroic, endangered,
regally rises

in spread-winged,
stainless-steel
splendor

from wavy grasses
lit with grasshopper,
snake and butterfly,

mud sparked
with barnacle, crab and clam.
Soundlessly

the crane's deep call
falls on these streets,
this once-marsh land.

Whooping Crane

A snowy-white bird with black wingtips, the whooping crane is the best-known endangered species in North America. It is the largest of North American birds, with a wingspan of 8 feet, a weight of up to 16 pounds, and a height up to 5 feet. It flies with its long neck stretched out straight and its long, thin legs trailing behind. The whooping crane's 2,400 mile migration route begins in wintering grounds in Texas, then crosses Oklahoma, Nebraska, South Dakota, North Dakota and Montana to its Arctic Circle summer home in Canada. Collision with power lines is the primary known cause of death, and chemical contamination from tanker spillage along the Gulf International Waterway also creates habitat hazards for the cranes. To ensure the health of whooping cranes, researches at Patuxent Wildlife Refuge Center in Maryland take eggs from the parents and hand-rear the young. Parent brooding sounds are played to the unhatched eggs, and after hatching, caretakers in crane costumes guide the chicks to food and water. Cranes learn to fly by running beside an ultralight plane, then flapping their wings when the plane lifts off; they also learn the migration route by following the plane.

Kent Ullberg (b. 1945), a Swedish sculptor specializing in wildlife art, realistically reproduces here not only the majestic bird, but also the saltwater Texas biotope of its winter habitat and the freshwater Arctic marshes of its summer home.

Kent Ullberg, Whooping Crane (Grus Americanus), 1986-89. Stainless steel. Courtyard of 1412 16th Street, NW (former National Wildlife Building), O Street entrance.

Timothy Parker

Louis Paul Jonas, *Uncle Beazley*, 1964. Fiberglass. In rhinoceros exhibit, National Zoo.

Timothy Parker

eXtinct Dinosaur

Triceratops (Latin for three-horned face) looks very friendly in this 1964 fiberglass sculpture by Louis Paul Jonas (1894-1971). Named Uncle Beazley for the dinosaur that hatched from an egg in the children's story, *The Enormous Egg*, the sculpture was originally created for the Sinclair Oil Company's exhibition for the 1964 New York State Fair. For many years, when it stood in front of the Museum of Natural History in Washington, children climbed up and slid down the sculpture. Now it grazes at the National Zoo with its relative, the rhinoceros.

Triceratops, a herding herbivore, lived during the Late Cretaceous period 72–65 million years ago. It was distinguished by its four sturdy legs, a large bone plate around its head, one horn above the nose and one above each eye. About 10 feet tall, 30 feet long, it weighed 6–12 tons.

eXtinct Dinosaur

Dust swirled, earth roared
as Triceratops,
last of the giant dinosaurs,
thundered in great herds
across the prairie.

Dimly, out of morning mist
a form appears. A ghost
of the past? No,
a replica of fiberglass,
head dipped to nibble grass.

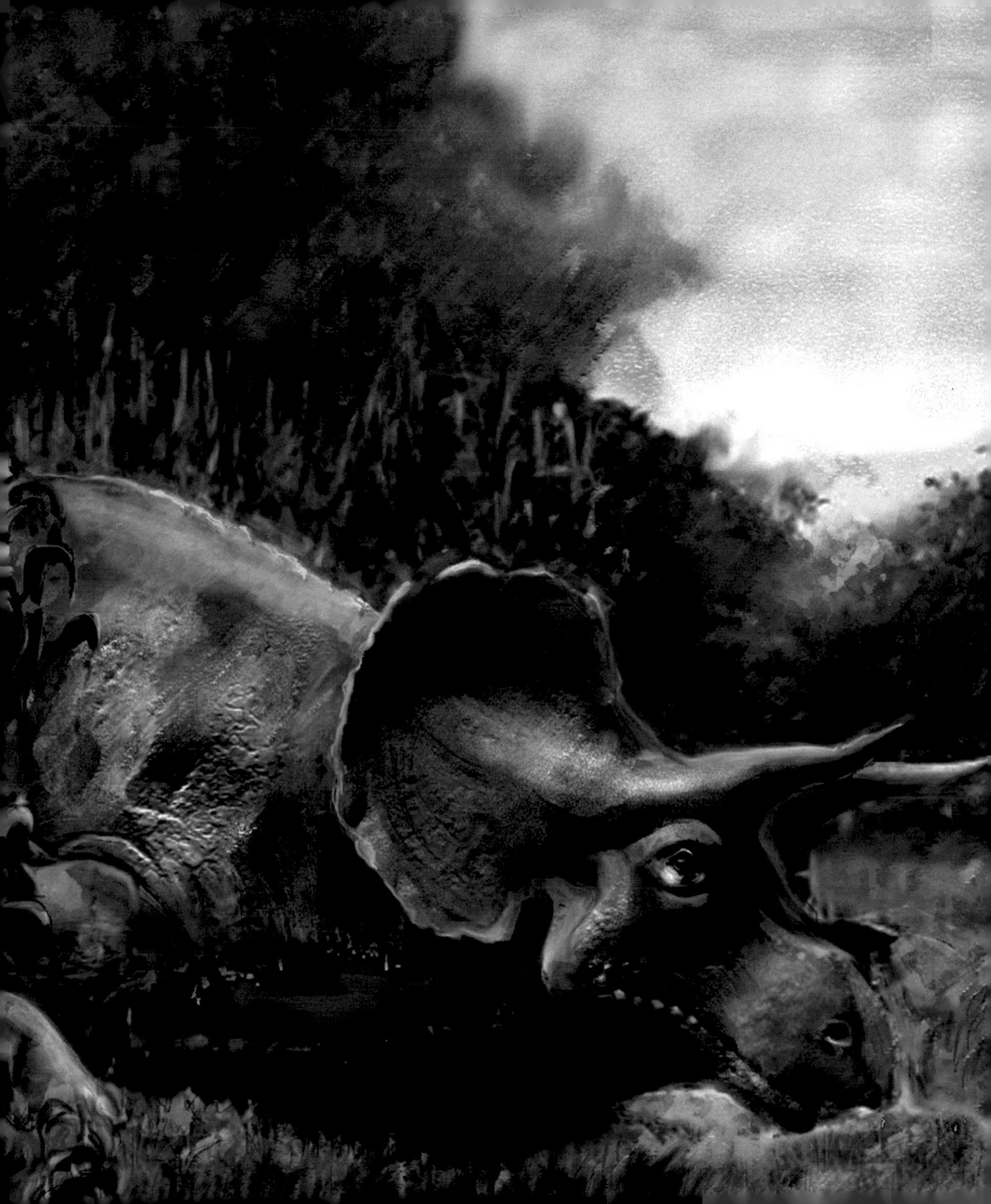

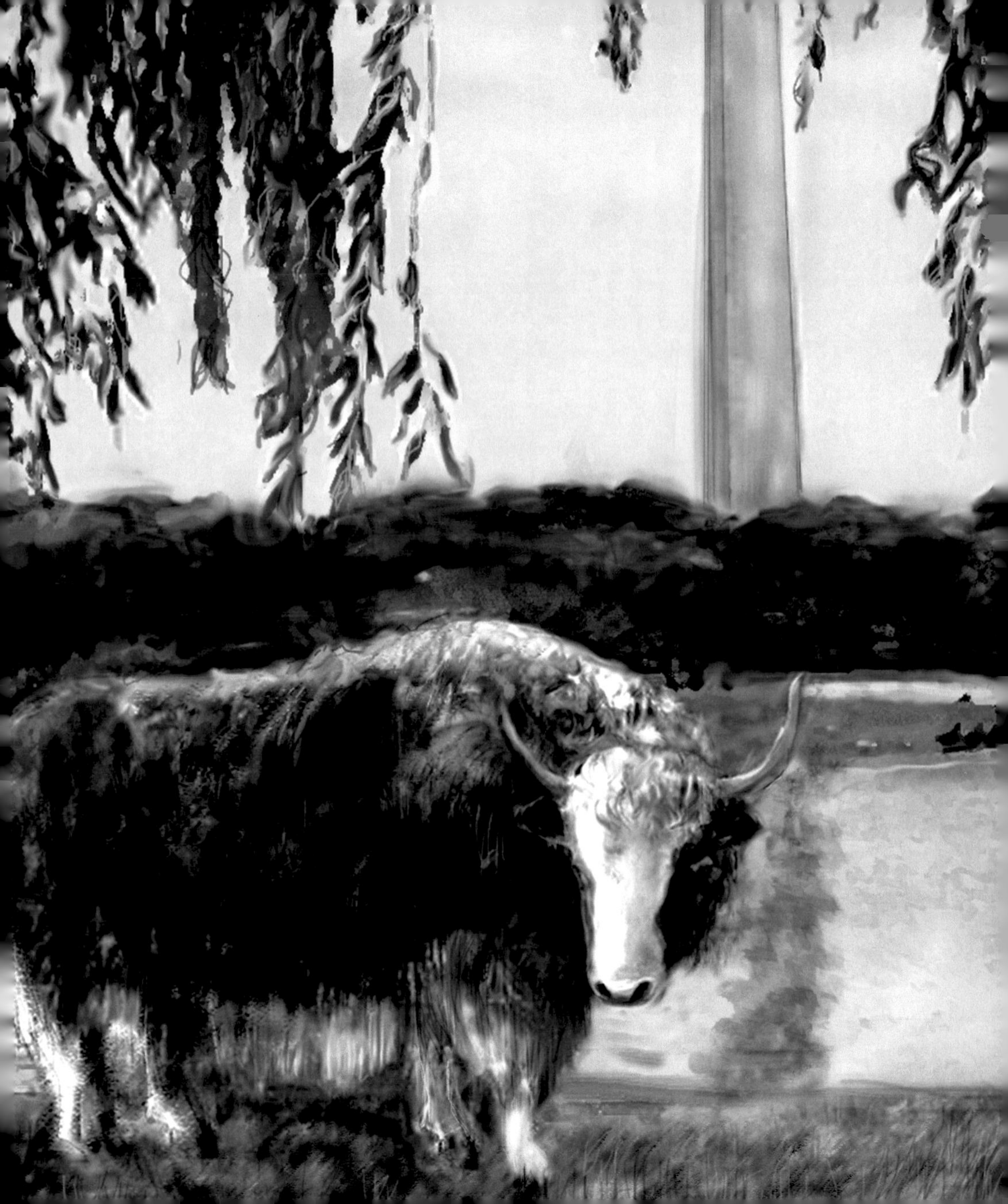

Yak

Shaggy majesty
of hair and horns
and high-humped back,
the wild yak
wanders Tibet's
cold plateaus,
its long, low grunt,
resounding far,
unanswered here
in Washington,
which lacks yaks.

Yak

No known sculpture.

The wild yak once ranged over the entire Tibetan plateau north of the Himalayas. With a thick coat, an ability to clamber nimbly over rough terrain, and a large lung capacity aided by the great number of blood cells which increases its oxygen-carrying ability, the yak is supremely adapted to its harsh environment. It lives on the grasses, herbs and lichen of the treeless plains at an altitude between 10,500 and 18,000 feet, the limit of vegetation. Probably domesticated during the 1st millennium B.C.E., domestic yaks provide wool, milk, yogurt, butter and meat for the nomadic Tibetan herders, who also use its dung for cooking fires and its bones for jewelry. Possibly extinct now in Nepal, the wild yak can be found in the plateaus and mountains of some areas of China and India. There are no known yak sculptures in Washington.

Zebra

Timothy Parker

Allan Herschell, Smithsonian Carousel, ca. 1947. 1000 Jefferson Drive, SW, in front of the Castle, National Mall.

The zebra shares with the horse and rhinoceros the distinction of being an odd-toed hoofed mammal. Primarily a grazer, with a body specialized for running, it roams the African plains. The three different species – Plains, Mountain and Desert (or Grevy's) – have an identifiable pattern of black and white stripes, but within the broader design, each individual zebra has a unique stripe pattern.

This carved zebra is part of the Smithsonian Carousel, probably a 1947 Allan Herschell half-and-half (referring to its wood and fiberglass construction), one of the last made by the Allan Herschell Company of North Tanawanda, New York. An earlier wooden Herschell carousel, now in Wheaton Regional Park in Montgomery County, Maryland, was first set up on the Mall in the 1960's. A Whirlitzer band organ provides the distinctive organ music associated with carousels.

The history of the carousel dates back to a Byzantine etching of 500 C.E. that portrays riders swinging in baskets tied to a central pole. The modern carousel dates from the mid-1800s in Europe, with wooden horses powered in a circle first by mule and later by engines. In the United States in the late 1800s, three main styles of carousel animal carving developed: the realistic and regal "Philadelphia" style of German immigrant Gustav Denzel, who built the first full-size carousel in America in 1870; the more fanciful and animated "Coney Island" established by Danish immigrant Charles I. D. Looff in 1876; and the later "Country Fair" style of simple figures on a portable carousel for use in traveling shows and country fairs. Local examples are the newly restored Denzel carousel at Glen Echo and the country fair carousel showcased during the Flower Mart at the National Cathedral. The wide popularity of carousels from the early 1880s to the 1930s created a "golden age" of gifted artists who carved magical carousel figures and engineers who brought mechanical innovations to the carousel. Today, a new generation of talented carvers is emerging as we have come to recognize the importance of the carousel in American history and culture.

Zebra

Around, around,
around, the carousel
beside the Castle whirls,
organ music skirling,
up and down, around,
around, one ticket
for a ride on horse
or swan or bear –
or the zebra there,
black and white
and proudly, joyfully
bounding through
this spinning world,
for a while ours.

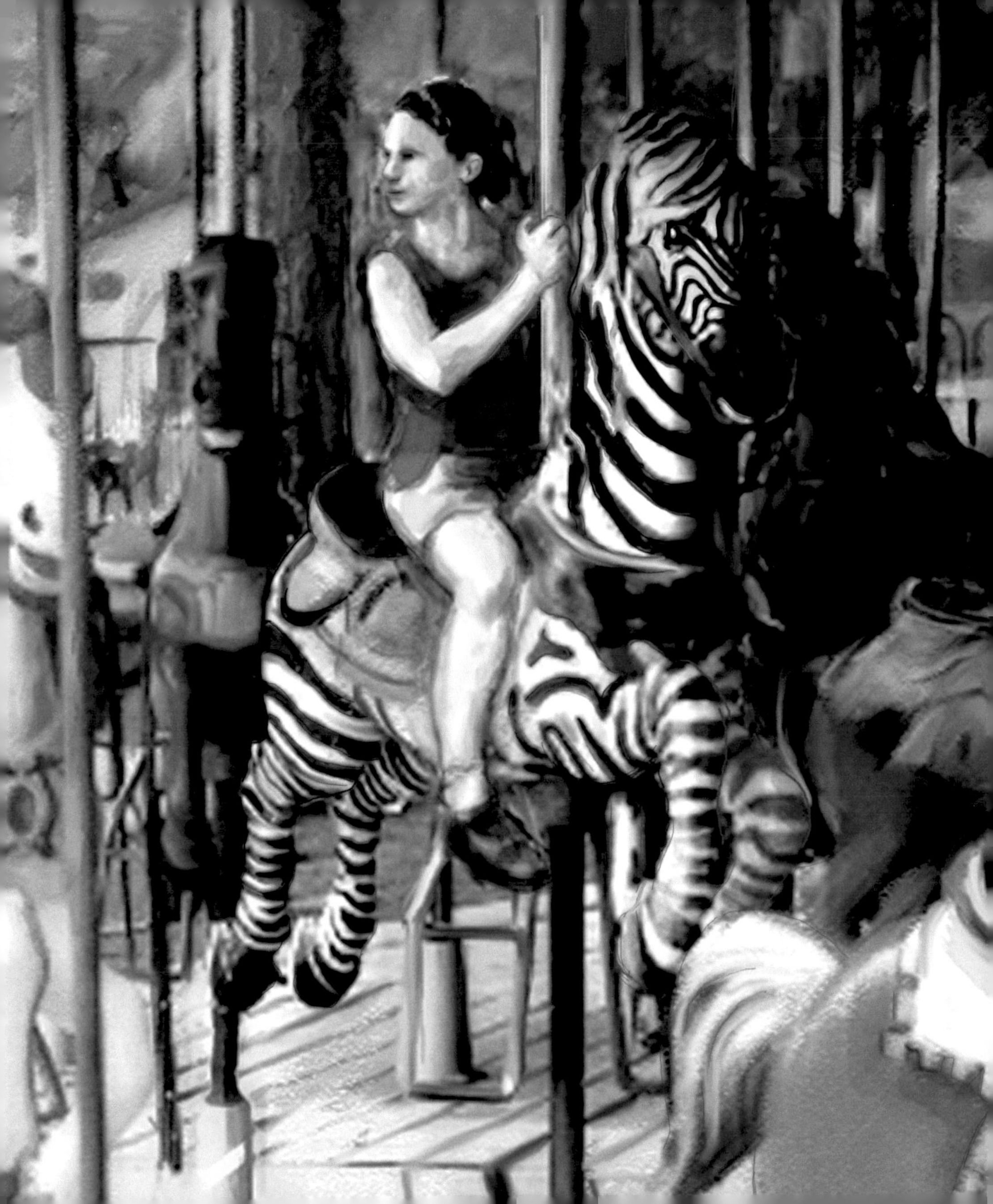

Locations

- **A** Anteater — National Zoo, in front of the Small Mammal House
- **B** Bison — Q Street Bridge at 24th Street, NW
- **C** Crab — Between Constitution & Pennsylvania Avenues near 10th Street, NW
- **D** Dog — FDR Memorial, Ohio Drive & Independence Avenue, SW
- **E** Elephant — Indian Embassy, 2536 Massachusetts Avenue, NW
- **F** Fawn — Judiciary Park, 5th & D Streets, NW
- **G** Gull — Lady Bird Johnson Park, George Washington Parkway
- **H** Hare — National Gallery of Art Sculpture Garden, Constitution Avenue at 7th Street, NW
- **I** Insect — John Marshall Park, C Street between 3rd & 4th Streets, NW
- **J** Jaguar — Art Museum of the Americas, 201 18th Street, NW
- **K** Kangaroo — Australian Embassy, 1601 Massachusetts Avenue, NW
- **L** Lion — Corcoran Gallery of Art, 17th Street & New York Avenue, NW
- **M** Mule — National Building Museum, 5th & F Streets, NW
- **N** Newt — Formerly at National Zoo
- **O** Owl — National Academy of Sciences, 2101 Constitution Avenue, SW
- **P** Penguin — Walter Reed Army Medical Center, Aspen Street between Georgia Avenue & 16th Street, NW
- **Q** Qing Dynasty Dragon — Friendship Arch, 7th & H Streets, NW
- **R** River Horse — George Washington University, 21st & I Streets, NW
- **S** Spider — National Gallery of Art Sculpture Garden
- **T** Turtle — Plaza of the United States Supreme Court, 1 First Street, NE
- **U** Unicorn — Unicorn Lane at Oregon Avenue, NW
- **V** Vietnamese Ox — Education Building foyer, east wall, National Zoo
- **W** Whooping Crane — Courtyard of 1412 16th Street, NW, O Street entrance
- **X** eXtinct Dinosaur — In rhinoceros exhibit, National Zoo
- **Y** Yak — No known address
- **Z** Zebra — 1000 Jefferson Drive, SW, in front of the Castle, National Mall

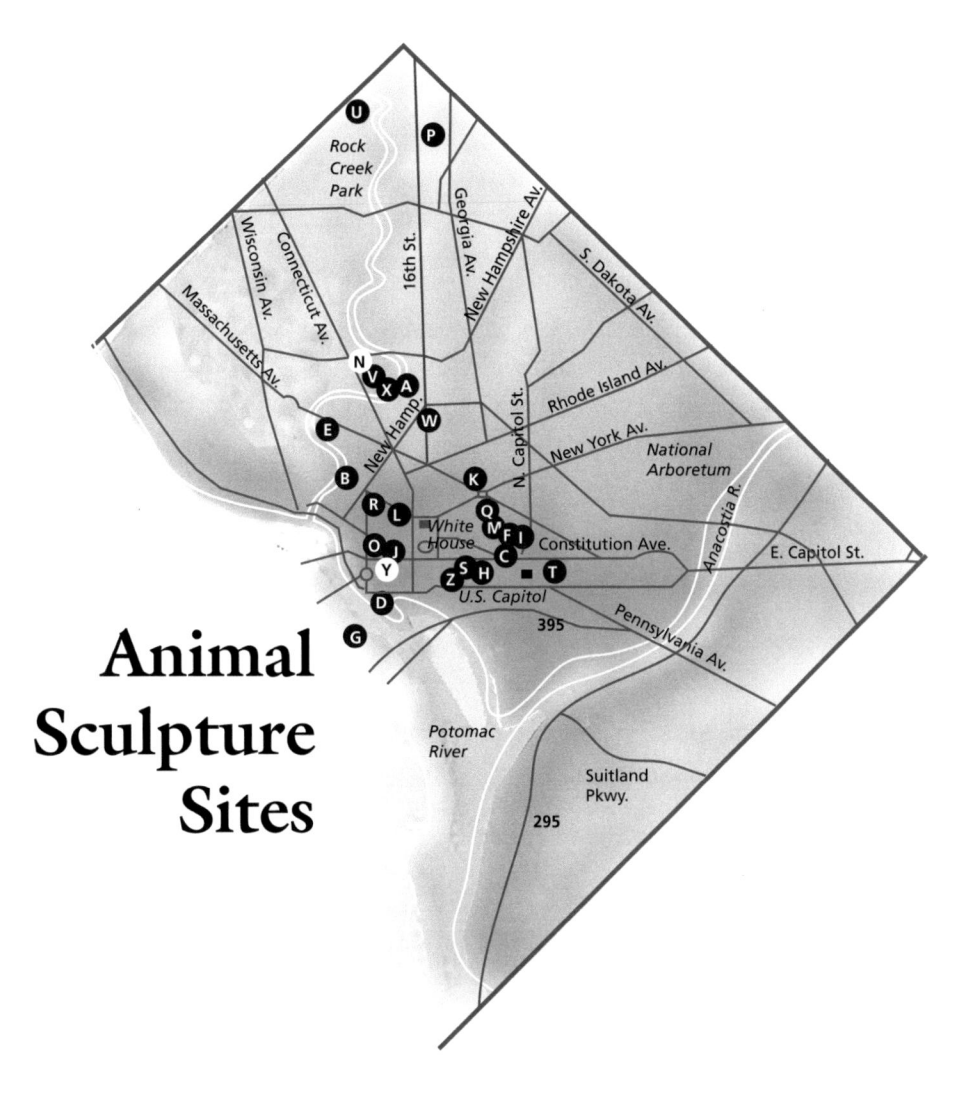

Animal Sculpture Sites

79

Zoo Notes

A selective list of other animal sculptures in DC: fairly inclusive lists for the National Zoo, the National Gallery of Art Sculpture Garden, and the Hirshhorn Sculpture Garden; a small representation of the dozens of animal gargoyles and grotesques of the National Cathedral; and a small number of the countless eagle sculptures, medallions and reliefs on government structures. Washington also hosts many temporary exhibits of animal art, such as the Party Animals, the Pandamania Pandas and a rotating sculpture exhibit of animal sculptures at the National Geographic Society.

American Wildlife

Lumen Martin Winter, *American Wildlife*, 1960. Carrera marble. 1412 16th Street, NW.
13 bas-relief panels of American wildlife figures, each panel representative of a different ecological region of the US.

Bee

Egyptian, Hieroglyphic Honeybee (reproduction), 2nd Millennium B.C.E. Concrete. Invertebrate House, National Zoo.

80

Bear

Cornelia Van A. Chapin, *Chapin Bear Cub,* 1952. Volcanic rock. Think Tank, National Zoo.

Laura Swing Kemeys, *Bear Cubs,* 1907. Cast stone. One of several finials, including bobcats and fox cubs, atop the Think Tank, National Zoo.

Jacob Lipkin, *Lipkin Bear Cub,* 1969. Porphyry. Major Bear Path near Lemur Island, National Zoo.

Heinz Warneke, *Wrestling Bears,* ca. 1935. Cast stone. Olmstead Walk, near Lion House Hill, National Zoo. The zoo booklet, "Art in The Park," names them *Tumbling Bears,* and notes they are made of granite.

Bird

Richard Hunt, *Seachange*, ca. 1984. Welded corten steel. Plaza near Library, University of the District of Columbia, 4200 Connecticut Avenue, NW. Author speculation of animal form based on name of UDC mascot, the Firebird.

Joan Miro, *Lunar Bird*, 1944-46, enlarged and cast in bronze, 1966-67. Hirshhorn Sculpture Garden, National Mall.

Bison

Anonymous. Metal. Galludet University. In front of the Field House, 600 Florida Avenue, NE. The bison is the school mascot.

Edwin Morris, *Animal Heads,* 1937. Painted cast iron. Department of Agriculture, North Building, Independence Avenue between 12th and 14th Streets, SW. See Turkey entry.

Butterfly

Joan Somworth and Corcoran ArtReach program, Mural, 2003. Tile mosaic. Education Center, Kenilworth Aquatic Garden, 1900 Anacostia Avenue, SE. See Dragonfly entry.

Cat

Anonymous. Argyle Terrace, 2201 22nd Street, NW (built ca. 1899), on the roof overlooking Massachusetts Avenue. There are many urban legends surrounding this cat. Actually, the first owner, the Miller family, never owned a cat. Young Townsend Miller admired this sculpture in a local artist's studio and was given the cat. Townsend's father then placed it on the roof of the family home. An arsonist's fire in 1984 gutted the house and the cat disappeared for a time. It was found months later partly buried in a neighbor's yard and was returned to the roof after the renovation.

Chimpanzee

Bart Walter, *The Gathering*, 2002. Think Tank Courtyard, National Zoo. Maryland artist Bart Walter combines close observation in the field with experience recalled in the studio in order, he says, "to capture the essence of a living being." The *Observer* is part of Walter's sculpture of a group of seven figures modelled on a typical chimpanzee social group, acting out roles of Ally, Alpha, Observer, Matriarch, Servant, Youth and Explorer.

Crane

Nina Akamu, cranes in barbed wire, *National Japanese American Memorial*, 2002. Bronze. Triangular park bounded by D Street, Louisiana and New Jersey Avenues, NW.

Henry Cogswell, *Temperance Fountain*, ca. 1880. Bronze. Pennsylvania Avenue and 7th Street, NW. Cogswell, a San Francisco dentist who made his money in real estate during the Gold Rush era, donated these fountains to many cities, including Boston and San Francisco. The water crane is a symbol of the purity of water over liquor. Note Dolphin entry.

Crocodile (family)

Anonymous, relief panel, ca. 1930s. Alban Towers, 3700 Massachusetts Avenue, NW.

Carl Tucker and Edward Ratti, gargoyle, ca. 1965. Limestone. Washington National Cathedral, South nave, outer aisle level. Wisconsin and Massachusetts Avenues, NW.

Dog

Anonymous, *Victor S. Blundon Monument*, 1936. Granite. Glenwood Cemetery, 2219 Lincoln Road, NE, Section F.

Anonymous, *St. Dominic*, ca. 1905. Marble. Dominican House of Studies, 487 Michigan Avenue, NE. The dog's foot on the globe symbolizes St. Dominic's mission to preach to the world.

James Earle Fraser, *The Recorder of the Archives*, 1935. Limestone. National Archives, Constitution Avenue, between 7th and 9th Streets, NW, on the pediment. Also note winged horse, and *Acroterion Eagles* on the upper corners of the pediment. On the Pennsylvania Avenue side, note *Destiny*, a pediment sculpture with eagles and horses by Adolph Alexander Weinman, 1935.

Dolphin

Henry Cogswell, *Temperance Fountain,* ca. 1880. Bronze. Pennsylvania Avenue and 7th Street, NW. See main entry for Crane.

Daniel Chester French, *Rear Admiral Samuel Francis Dupont Memorial Fountain*, 1921. Marble. Dupont Circle, Massachusetts Avenue and Connecticut Avenue, NW. Dupont was the first Union naval hero of the Civil War. See Gull entry.

Charles Henry Niehaus, *Commodore John Paul Jones Memorial*, 1912. Marble. West Potomac Park, Independence Avenue and 17th Street, SW. Jones, the father of the US Navy, is credited with the declaration, "I have not yet begun to fight!"

Albert Weinert, *The Court of Neptune Fountain*, 1897-98. Granite. Library of Congress Main Building, First Street, between Independence Avenue and East Capitol Street, SE. Main fountain sculpture and design by Roland Hinton Perry. See Triton entry.

Donkey

John Gregory, *Scenes from Shakespeare*, 1932. Marble. Folger Shakespeare Library, East Capitol and 2nd Streets, SE. This panel shows the transformation of Bottom, the tailor, in *A Midsummer Night's Dream*.

Dove

Gordon Kray, *Kahlil Gibran Memorial Park*, 1990. Massachusetts Avenue, NW, in the 3100 block, across from the British Embassy. Kahlil Gibran was a Lebanese-born Arab-American writer, artist and philosopher.

Richard Hunt, *Freedman's Column*, 1989. Howard University. Welded bronze. Author speculation on animal form.

Dragon

Anonymous, ca. 1930s. Apartment building entrance, 2029 Connecticut Avenue, NW.

DRAGON
Smithmeyer and Pelz (architects), Downspout, ca. 1900. Copper. Healy Hall, Georgetown University. 37th and O Streets, NW. Healy Hall, designed in the Flemish Renaissance style of symmetrical composition and rounded arches, was constructed between 1887 and 1909. The architects also designed the Jefferson Building of the Library of Congress.

Dragonfly
Joan Somworth and Corcoran ArtReach Program, Mural, 2003. Tile mosaic. Education Building, Kenilworth Aquatic Gardens, 1900 Anacostia Avenue, SE. Note butterfly entry. Note also kingfisher and turtle on mural.

Eagle
Anonymous, Art Deco-style eagle, ca. 2000. Entrance steps, Municipal Center, 300 Indiana Avenue, NW. Designed to conform to the 1941 Nathan C. Wyeth Art Deco building design.

Anonymous, ca. 1870s. Gate 1, St. Elizabeth's Hospital, 2700 Martin Luther King, Jr. Avenue, SE.

EAGLE
Little & Brown, Architects (designer), *The Society of the Cincinnati Pediment*, 1905. Marble. Anderson House, 2118 Massachusetts Avenue, NW. The society formed by Revolutionary War officers was named for Roman leader Cincinnatus who defeated the barbarians, resigned his dictatorship and returned to farming.

Ernest C. Bairstow, *Bairstow Eagle Lampposts*, 1906. Iron. Taft Bridge, Connecticut Avenue, NW. Other examples of Bairstow's work can be found on the Old City Post Office Building and the Lincoln Memorial.

L. G. Isard and W. T. Matia, AU Eagle, 1997. Outside Bender Arena, American University, off Massachusetts Avenue, NW. Inscribed on the plaque are the words, *Once an eagle, always an eagle.*

Raymond J. Kaskey, World War II Memorial Eagles, 2004. Bronze. World War II Memorial, National Mall, east end of Reflecting Pool between the Lincoln Memorial and the Washington Monument. Kaskey sculpted all the bronze symbols at the memorial. See also entry for National Law Enforcement Lions.

EAGLE
Joseph Younger, Eagles, ca. 1932. Granite. Kennedy-Warren Apartment Building, 3133 Connecticut Avenue, NW. Also note high-relief elephants, *Geometric Eagles* above main entrance, and griffins on the top of the building. Between the World Wars, many apartment houses between 2100 and 3900 Connecticut Avenue employed Art Deco designs, characterized by geometric patterns and Islamic, Egyptian or medieval architectural motifs. This building is an example of Aztec Art Deco. The final wing of the original Kennedy-Warren design was completed in 2004.

Anonymous, 1912. Union Station, Massachusetts and Delaware Avenues, NE.

David H. Turner, *Eagle*, ca. 1995. Bronze. Garden outside Bird House, National Zoo.

EAGLE
Adolph Alexander Weinman, *Pennsylvania Railroad Eagle*, 1910. Tennessee marble. Outside Bird House, National Zoo. Weinman sculpted 22 of these eagles for the old Penn Station Railroad building in New York City. Each eagle, weighing 5700 pounds, was sculpted from pink marble chosen to match the pink granite of Penn Station.

Elephant

Jimilu Mason, *Baby Elephant Fountain*, 1990. Bronze. Outside Elephant House, National Zoo.

Robyn Rogers, *Metrophant*, 2002. Painted fiberglass. Martin Luther King Memorial Library, 901 G Street, NW. One of the winning designs for The Party Animals contest sponsored by The DC Commission on the Arts to raise money for the city.

Equestrian Statue

Clark Mills, *Lieutenant General George Washington*, 1860. Bronze. Washington Circle, Pennsylvania Avenue, New Hampshire Avenue, 23rd and K Streets, NW. Washington boasts over 25 equestrian statues, one of the most popular memorial forms of the mid-19th century. Mills is considered one of the greatest equestrian statue sculptors. His most famous statue is of Andrew Jackson, in Lafayette Park in front of the White House.

Fish

Enrique Monjo, Biblical Figure, 1962. Limestone. South Transept Portal, Washington National Cathedral, Wisconsin and Massachusetts Avenues, NW.

C. Brooke Lamm, *Fish Bone*, 1992. Metal. Exterior wall, Amazonia, National Zoo.

Frog

John Joseph Earley, *Two Frogs In a Pond*, 1931. Stone sculptural relief. Reptile Discovery Center, National Zoo.

William Mozart McVey, *Happy Frog*, 1975. Bronze. Across from Reptile Discovery Center, National Zoo. Another important contemporary frog sculpture is Jim Henson's *Kermit the Frog* at the University of Maryland in College Park.

Roland Hinton Perry, *The Court of Neptune Fountain*, 1897-98. Bronze. Library of Congress Main Building, First Street, SE, between Independence Avenue and East Capitol Street. See entries for Horse and Triton.

Kim Shaklee, *Hop To It*, 1999. Bronze. Across from Education Building, National Zoo.

Gargoyle

Anonymous, 1895. Andrew Rankin Memorial Chapel, Howard University, 2365 6th Street, NW. Dr. Martin Luther King, Jr., Eleanor Roosevelt and John F. Kennedy spoke in this historic gothic-style chapel.

Giraffe

Anonymous. *Giraffe Rock Art*, recent cast of 7,000-year-old rock carving from Niger. Aluminum. Courtyard, National Geographic Society, 1145 17th Street, NW.

Gorilla

William Klapp, *Gorilla Family*, 1980. Fiberglass. Behind Great Ape House, National Zoo. See entry for Orangutan.

Griffin

Anonymous, concrete bench on Independence Avenue, SE, between First Street and 2nd Street, SE.

GRIFFIN
Paul Philippe Cret, architect. Federal Reserve Board Building, Constitution Avenue and 20th Street, NW, balcony on C Street. In Greek myth, a griffin, which has the head and wings of an eagle and the body of a lion, guarded the gold stores at Scythia.

Edmond Romulus Amateis, *Acacia Griffins*, 1936. Limestone. 51 Louisiana Avenue, NW. One male and one female griffin. Named for the Acacia Mutual Life Insurance Company, former owner of the building, which adopted the griffin as its symbol.

Gull

Daniel Chester French, *Rear Admiral Samuel Francis Dupont Memorial Fountain: The Sea*, 1921. Marble. Dupont Circle, Massachusetts and Connecticut Avenues, NW. See Dolphin entry.

Hare

Barry Flanagan, *The Drummer*, 1996. Bronze. Hirshhorn Museum plaza, National Mall.

95

Heron

Charles Bulfinch (architect and designer of Capitol grounds), ca. 1826. Sandstone. United States Capitol Building, fountain in wall along First Street, NW.

Horse

Marino Marini, *Horse and Rider*, 1952-53. Bronze. Hirshhorn Museum Sculpture Garden, National Mall.

Leo Friedlander, *The Arts of War: Valor*, designed 1925, cast 1949, erected 1951. Gilded bronze. West Potomac Park, Lincoln Memorial Circle, SW, entrance to Arlington Memorial Bridge. One of a pair of Neoclassical figures, and companion to Fraser's *Arts of Peace*.

James Earle Fraser, *The Arts of Peace: Aspiration and Literature*, designed 1925, cast 1949, erected 1951. Gilded bronze. West Potomac Park, Lincoln Memorial Circle, SW, entrance to Rock Creek Parkway. One of a pair extolling the fine arts. Fraser designed the Buffalo Nickel in 1913.

HORSE
Roland Hinton Perry, *The Court of Neptune Fountain*, 1897-98. Bronze. Library of Congress Main Building, First Street, between Independence and East Capitol Street, SE. Note turtle and snake in lower area. See entry for Triton.

Michael Lantz, *Man Controlling Trade*, 1942. Limestone. Federal Trade Commission, 6th Street between Pennsylvania and Constitution Avenues, NW. Lantz, a young WPA instructor, worked in the heroic 1930s Art Deco style.

John Gregory, winged horse, 1932. Marble. Folger Shakespeare Library, East Capitol and 2nd Streets, SE. In ancient Greek myth, poets sought inspiration by riding on the back of Pegasus. See also Pegasus atop the memorial to Pushkin at George Washington University at 22nd and I Street, NW.

HORSE

Henry Merwin Shrady, *General Ulysses S. Grant Memorial*, 1922. Bronze. Union Square, east end of the Mall. Shrady devoted over twenty years of intense effort to this memorial. In order to understand the life of the soldiers, he served for four years in the National Guard. To learn the muscle structure of horses, he dissected horse cadavers. Note the powerful portrayals of Cincinnatus, Grant's horse, and the others pulling the caisson. Perhaps Shrady's personal connection with Grant (Shrady's father was the physician attending Grant in his final days) accounts for some of the power of this memorial.

Anonymous, horse heads, ca. 1890. Ceramic. 1111 34th Street, NW. These horseheads were moved from their original location on the Heurich Brewing Company stables in Foggy Bottom when the buildings were razed in 1969 to make way for the Kennedy Center. During the company's early years, horse-drawn carriages were used to deliver specialty beer products created from recipes Christian Heurich brought with him from Germany. With money from his business, Heurich was able to build a mansion in Dupont Circle. See Salamander entry.

Lion

Anonymous. British Embassy. 3100 Massachusetts Avenue, NW. See Unicorn entry.

LION
Henry Merwin Shrady, *General Ulysses S. Grant Memorial*, 1922. Bronze. Union Square, east end of the Mall, near reflecting pool. See Horse entry for Grant Memorial.

Roland Hinton Perry, *Perry Lions*. Bronze. National Zoo Entrance, Connecticut Avenue, NW. See cover description for Taft Bridge Lions. Cast in 2002 from original 1906 precast concrete sculptures.

Anonymous, mythological lion. Entrance, Embassy of People's Republic of China, 2300 Connecticut Avenue, NW.

Lorado Z. Taft, *Columbus Fountain*, 1912. Marble. Union Station Plaza, Massachusetts and Delaware Avenues, SW. Also note the four eagles that support the globe on top of the monument.

LION
Raymond J. Kaskey, lions protecting cubs, 1991. Bronze. *National Law Enforcement Officers Memorial*, Judiciary Square, E Street between 4th and 5th Streets, NW. This sculpture symbolizes the protective role of law officers in the community. Kaskey also designed the eagles for the WW II memorial. See Eagle entry.

Antonio Francisco Lisboa, *The Prophet Daniel*, 1962. Concrete. Pan American Union Building, Constitution Avenue and 17th Street, NW. Replica of the original 1805 soapstone carving by Lisboa, the first important Brazilian sculptor. The twelve original prophets in Lisboa's Brazilian Baroque style decorate a church in Conqonhardo Campo, Brazil.

Lizard
John Joseph Earley, *Reptile Portal*, 1931. Stone. Reptile Discovery Center, National Zoo.

John Joseph Earley, *Reptile Portal*, 1931. Stone. Reptile Discovery Center, National Zoo. One of a pair of giant lizards on the upper section of the gabled porch. Also note the small reptile relief panels on the arch and the turtles and toads of the porch columns. See Turtle and Toad entries for John Joseph Earley.

LIZARD

Charles R. Knight, two giant lizards. Reptile Discovery Center, smaller door to right of main entrance, National Zoo.

Llama

Anonymous, shield of Peru. Painted metal. Medallion on gate, Embassy of Peru Residence, Garrison and 30th Streets, NW.

Mammoth

Charles R. Knight, *Mammoth and Mastodon*s, ca. 1934. Stone relief. Elephant House, left entrance, National Zoo.

Monkey

Evelyn M. Haller, *Togetherness*, 1992. Bronze. Golden Lion Tamarin Exhibit, inside Small Mammal House, National Zoo.

Mythical Creatures
Bill Reid, *The Spirit of Haida Gwaii* (or *The Black Canoe*), ca. 1996. Bronze. Embassy of Canada, 501 Pennsylvania Avenue, NW.

Octopus
William Klapp, *Octopus*, 1985. Steel. Invertebrate House, above entrance, National Zoo.

Orangutan
William Klapp, *Orang*, 1987-88. Fiberglass. Great Ape House, above exit, National Zoo. See entry for Gorilla.

Owl
Anonymous, ca. 1927. Alban Towers, above entrance, 3700 Massachusetts Avenue, NW. An example of Gothic or Tudor Revival architecture. Note also terra cotta relief of pig and swan on entryway.

Panda

Phillip Ratner, *Giant Panda*, 1993. Painted metal. Panda Plaza, National Zoo. A memorial to Ling Ling, a giant panda that lived at the zoo from 1972-92.

Parrot

Anonymous, *Parrots*, ca. 1930. Limestone. 2101 Connecticut Avenue, NW. Art Deco apartment building with Islamic arches and medieval motifs. Also note lion head medallions above the arched entry.

Polar Bear

I. T. Verdin Company, *Pelzman Glockenspiel*, 1976. Olmstead Walk, base of Lion and Tiger Hill, National Zoo. Note elephant, giraffe, and lion.

Rabbit

Dominico Mortellito, *Pied Piper 2*, 1936. Cast aluminum. Small Mammal House, inside, near exit, National Zoo. See Rat entry.

Ram

W. H. Livingston, Sr., *Greek Vases*, 1964. Marble. Rayburn Office Building, Independence Avenue between South Capitol and First Streets, SW. In Greek mythology, the horn of the goat that suckled Zeus broke off and became filled with fruit. This cornucopia is modeled after classical Greek sculpture of the horn of plenty.

Rat

Dominico Mortellito, *Pied Piper 1,* 1936. Cast aluminum. Small Mammal House, inside entrance, National Zoo. See Rabbit entry.

Salamander

Anonymous. Lightning rod, 1894. Heurich House, 1307 New Hampshire Avenue, NW. In art, the salamander symbolizes endurance. See entry for Horse Heads. Note also salamanders on terra cotta facade of apartment building at 2029 Connecticut Avenue, NW.

Sea Lion

S. Christine Smith, *Walrus, Seals, Sea Lions,* 1978. Ceramic relief. Sea Lion Pool, National Zoo. Note other sea mammals.

Snake

Anonymous, caduceus. Howard University College of Dentistry, 620 W Street, NW. Above entrance. Carried by Hermes, the messenger of the gods, the caduceus, a winged staff entwined by two serpents, is a symbol of the medical profession.

Sphinx

Adolph Alexander Weinman, *Masonic Sphinxes*, 1915. Limestone. Scottish Rite Freemason's Temple, 16th and S Streets, NW. The sphinx, a statue with the head of a man and the body of a lion, represents wisdom and power. The oldest surviving example is the huge sphinx on the banks of the Nile in Giza, Egypt, near Cairo, erected ca. 2550 B.C.E.

Starfish

Lucilda Dassardo, with the technical assistance of Attiya Debra Melton and students of Hyde Elementary School, *Under-water World*, 1992. Tile Mosaic. Anthony Hyde Elementary School, 3219 O Street, NW. Joint project of Filmore Arts Center and Hyde Elementary School. Note other sea creatures.

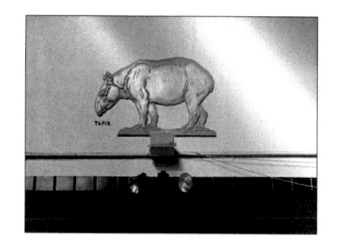

Tapir

Charles R. Knight, ca. 1936. Aluminum. One of 12 aluminum panels in the Elephant House, on the interior walls above the cages, National Zoo. Note also the mosaic medallions on the floor and the stone relief above the Elephant House entrance. See entry for Lizard; Knight designed the dinosaur mosaic for the *Reptile Portal*.

Tiger

Alexander Phimister Proctor, *Proctor's Tigers*, 1910. Bronze. 16th Street, Piney Branch Bridge, NW. Commissioned to be made of concrete, the tigers were instead cast in more durable bronze by Proctor. See also Bison in main text section.

Toad

John Joseph Earley, *Reptile Portal*, 1931. Reptile Discovery Center, National Zoo. See Lizard and Tortoise entries for John Joseph Earley.

Tortoise

John Joseph Earley, *Reptile Portal*, 1931. Reptile Discovery Center, National Zoo. See Lizard entry for John Joseph Earley.

Triton

Roland Hinton Perry, *The Court of Neptune Fountain*, 1897-98. Bronze. In Greek myth, Triton, the son of Neptune, had a man's head and torso and the lower body of a fish. The nymphs in the fountain sculpture represent the Nereids, daughters of Nereus, the "wise old man of the sea." Although Nereids generally ride dolphins, here they ride sea horses, wild creatures with the body of a horse and the tail of a fish. Note also the bronze frog, snake and dolphin water spouts. See Dolphin entry for Albert Weinert.

Turkey

Edwin Morris, *Animal Heads*, 1937. Painted cast iron. Department of Agriculture, South Building, Independence Avenue, between 14th and 12th Streets, SW. One of several hundred relief panels. In the 1780s Benjamin Franklin nominated the turkey as the official bird of the United States for its superior intelligence.

Turtle

Frédéric Auguste Bartholdi, *Bartholdi Fountain*, 1976. Cast iron. US Botanical Garden, Independence Avenue and First Street, SW. During the late 19th century, this fountain with its display of twelve electric lights was a major attraction. Bartholdi also designed the *Statue of Liberty*.

Unicorn

Anonymous, British Embassy. 3100 Massachusetts Avenue, NW. See Lion entry, British Embassy.

Wolf

Mark Rossi, *Female Wolf and Pups,* 2004. National Defenders of Wildlife. 1130 17th Street, NW. Although his work is realistic, Arizona artist Mark Rossi, son of western artist Paul Rossi, likes to allow his forms freedom "to emerge from the clay and metal." Notice also the stained glass panels of animals in the entry lobby.

Bibliography

Books:

Applewhite, E. J. *Washington Itself: An Informal Guide to the Capital of the United States.* Lanham, Maryland: Madison Books, 1981; 1993.

Gasch, Wendy True. *Guide to Gargoyles and Other Grotesques.* Washington, DC: Washington National Cathedral, 2003.

Forgey, Benjamin. *Washington: Scenes from a Capital City.* Singapore: Editions Didier Millet, 2003.

Goode, James M. *The Outdoor Sculpture of Washington, DC : A Comprehensive Historical Guide.* Washington, DC: Smithsonian Institution Press, 1974.

_____. *Best Addresses: A Century of Washington's Most Distinguished Apartment Houses.* Washington, DC and London: Smithsonian Institution Press, 2003.

Scott, Pamela and Antoinette J. Lee. *Buildings of the District of Columbia.* New York and Oxford: Oxford University Press, 1993.

Smithsonian Institution. *Official Guide to the Smithsonian.* Washington, DC: Smithsonian Institution Press, 2002.

Informational Booklets, Brochures and Articles:

Forgey, Benjamin. "Hidden Treasures," *The Washington Post,* passim.

Friends of the National Zoo, Smithsonian Institution, National Zoological Park. "Art in the Park: Art as an Expression of Life", ca. 2000.

National Gallery of Art. "National Gallery of Art Sculpture Garden."

National Wildlife Federation. "The Story of Our Marble Panels" in "National Wildlife Federation," a pamphlet on the original headquarters of the federation at 1412 Sixteenth Street, NW, in Washington, DC, ca. 1961.

Organization of American States, "Art Museums of the Americas," 2000.

Richard, Paul. "From the Collection: Washington's Prize Possessions," *The Washington Post,* passim.

Sculptor/Architect

Akamu, Nina 84
Amateis, Edmond Romulus 95

Bass, Thomas 32
Bairstow, Ernest C. 89
Bartholdi, Frédéric Auguste 107
Bourgeois, Louise 56-57
Buberl, Casper 38
Bulfinch, Charles (architect and designer), 96

Canova, Antonio 32-33
Chapin, Cornelia Van A. 81
Cogswell, Henry 84, 86
Corbet, Harvey W. (architect) 20
Cret, Paul Philippe (architect) 27, 95

Dassardo, Lucilda 105
del Piatta, Ernesto Begni, 20
Denzel, Gustav 75

Enfield Pottery, 27
Earley, John Joseph 100, 106
Eggers, Otto R. (architect and designer) 8
Estern, Neil 9

Flagg, Ernest 33
Flanagan, Barry 21, 95
Fraser, James Earle 85, 96
French, Daniel Chester 86, 95
Friedlander, Leo 96

Gavaert, Jeanne 62-63
Gregory, John 8, 97

Haller, Evelyn M. 101
Haseltine, Herbert 2
Hunt, Richard 82, 87

Isard, L. G. 89

Jennewein, Carl Paul 14-15
Jimenez, Luis, i
Jonas, Louis Paul 69

Kaskey, Raymond J. 89, 100
Kelsey, Albert 27
Kemeys, Laura Swing 81
Klapp, William 94 102
Knight, Charles R. 101, 105
Kray, Gordon 87

Lamm, C. Brooke 92
Lantz, Michael 97
Lawrie, Lee 44
Lipkin, Jacob 81
Lisboa, Antonio Francisco 100
Little & Brown (designer) 89
Liu, Alfred 50
Livingston, Sr., W. H. 104
Looff, Charles I. D. 75

MacNeil, Herman Atkins 57
Manship, Paul 2
Marini, Marino 96
Mason, Jimilu 91
Matia, W. T. 89
McVey, William Mozart 93
Mills, Clark 92
Miro, Joan 82
Monjo, Enrique 92
Morris, Edwin 82, 107
Mortellito, Dominico 103, 104

Niehaus, Charles Henry 86

Perry, Roland Hinton cover art, i, 86, 93, 97, 99, 107

Proctor, Alexander Phimister 2-3, 106
Phillips, David 26

Ratti, Edward 84
Ratner, Phillip 103
Reid, Bill 102
Reinaldo i
Rodin, Auguste 21
Rogers, Robyn 91
Rossi, Mark 108

Saint-Gaudens, Louis 44
Shaklee, Kim 93
Shrady, Henry Merwin 98, 99
Smith, S. Christine 104
Somworth, Joan 83, 88
Smithmyer and Palz 88
Springweiler, Erwin Frederick 2

Taft, Lorado i, 89, 99
Tucker, Carl Z. 84
Turner, David H. 90

Ullberg, Kent 68

Verdin Company, I. T. 103

Walter, Bart 83
Warneke, Heinz 81
Waugh, Sidney Biehler, 8
Weinert, Albert 86, 107
Weinman, Adolph Alexander 85, 91, 105
Weitzman, Steven, 39
Whitney, H. P. 27
Winter, Lumen Martin, 80

Younger, Joseph, 90

Animals

American Wildlife, 80
Amphibian 39, 4
Ant 1
Anteater x, 1, 2, 78
Antelope 50
Arachnid 56
Arthropod 56

Badger 9
Barnacle 67
Bear 76, 81, 103
Beast 40
Bee 80
Bird 40, 44, 68, 82, 90, 107
Bison 2-3, 4, 5, 78, 82
Bobcat 81
Buffalo 3
Butterfly 67, 83

Cat 27, 83
Cetacean 50
Chimpanzee 83
Clam 67
Cobra 46
Cow i, 50
Crab 6, 7, 8-9, 67, 78
Crane 66, 67, 68, 78, 84
Crocodile 84

Deer 15, 48, 50
Dinosaur 57, 68-69, 70, 71, 78
Dog 9, 10, 11, 78, 85
Dolphin 50, 84, 86, 107
Donkey 37, 38, 87
Dove 87
Dragon 48, 49, 50, 78, 87-88
Dragonfly 24, 25, 26, 88
Duckling 45

Eagle 80, 85, 88-91, 95, 99, 100
Elephant 13, 14, 78, 91, 101, 103, 105
Emu 30, 31, 32
Equestrian statue 92

Fawn 14,15, 16, 17, 78
Fish 7, 26, 92, 107
Fox 9, 81
Frog 26, 28, 93, 107

Gargoyle 80, 84, 94
Giraffe 94, 103
Gorilla 94
Grasshopper 67
Griffin 90, 94-95
Grus Americanus 66, 67, 68
Gull 18, 19, 20, 78, 95

Hare 21, 22, 78, 95
Herbivore 68-69, 70, 71
Heron 96
Hippopotamus 50-51, 52
Horse i, 37, 38, 50, 52, 61, 74, 75, 76, 78, 85, 96-98, 107
Human 14, 22, 39, 40
Insect 1, 2, 24, 25, 26, 39, 56, 78

Jaguar 2, 27-28, 29, 78

Kangaroo 30, 31-32, 78
Kouprey 62-63, 64, 65

Lion i, 32-33, 34, 35, 44, 78, 95, 98-100, 101, 103, 105
Lizard 100-101
Llama 101
Lynx 43

Mammoth 101
Marsupial 30, 31, 32
Mite 56
Monkey 101
Mosquitoes 25, 45
Mule 36, 37-38, 75, 78
Mustang i, 3, 28
Myrmecophagidae 1
Mythical creatures 102

Newt 39, 40, 41, 78
Nymphs 107

Octopus 102
Orangutan 102
Owl 42, 43-44, 78, 102
Ox 62-63, 64, 65, 78

Panda 80, 103
Parrot 103
Penguin 44-45, 46, 47, 78
Pig 102
Polar Bear 103
Porpoise 50
Puma 2

Quarter horse frontispiece, i
Qing Dynasty Dragon 48, 49, 50, 78

Rabbit 21, 103
Ram 7, 104
Raptor 44
Rat 104
Reptile 57
Rhinoceros 69, 74
River horse 50-51, 52, 53, 78

111

Salamander 40, 104
Scottish terrier 9
Scorpion 56
Sea horses 107
Sea lion 104
Serpent 28, 43, 44, 105
Sheep 50
Snake 8, 67, 97, 105, 107
Spider 39, 54, 55, 56-57, 78
Sphinx 105
Stallion 37
Starfish 105
Swan 76, 102

Tapir 105
Termite 1, 2
Terrapin 57
Tick 56
Tiger 3, 106
Toad 100, 106
Tortoise 57
Triceratops 68-69, 70, 71
Triton 107
Turkey 82, 107
Turtle 57, 58, 59, 78, 88, 97, 100, 107

Unicorn 60, 61, 62, 78, 108

Vietnamese Ox 62-63, 64, 65, 78

Whale 50
Whooping Crane 66, 67, 68, 78
Wolf 108

eXtinct dinosaur 68-69, 70, 71, 78

Yak 72, 73, 74, 78

Zebra 74-75, 76, 77, 78

Duotones Printed by Stephenson MicroDot
Stephenson Printing Inc
Alexandria, Virginia
703-642-9000 • 800-336-4637